The "How to" of Debate

Skills and theories
for policy debate

T. Russell Hanes

A speech has two parts.
You must state your case, and you must prove it.

~ Aristotle, *Rhetoric*, c. 350 B.C.E.

Skills

Affirmative

Negative

Rhetoric

Any book, even a modest one such as this, does not happen without the help of quite a lot of people. I am indebted to:

Erin Dysart for copyediting;
Bryan Kraft for his kind comments on the first draft;
Stephen Pilson for his careful editing of the final draft;
Scott Devoid for providing an orientation for the book: the attitudes that differentiate novice debaters from experienced debaters;
Jason Brooks and Jason Peterson for many of the techniques for teaching speaking skills;
Owen Zahorcak, especially for his flow for the second chapter, his ideas on counterplan theory, his notes on common novice misconceptions, our discussions, and his editing, which helped me to craft much of the theoretical language;
Chuck Ballingall for gamely trusting me to teach unorthodox lesson plans, and the 2002–2003 Damien debaters, who were the brave guinea pigs to read experimental proto-chapters;
Chris Richter and the Portland State debate team for organizing various debate workshops and inviting me to lecture on debate theory and skills.

And as I was once a student myself, I owe a large debt of gratitude to my coaches throughout the years: Tom Black, Naveen Parti, Chuck Owens, Jon Barrow, Will Baker, Joe Patrice, and most especially my coach and friend, Dr. Alan Dove. I would also like to thank Braden Boucek, whose deft team leadership kept me in the activity at an early stage of discouragement.

Finally, I would like to beg the forgiveness of my family and friends for their perpetual tolerance of this odd hobby. Chase Lubbock, Emma Gray, Jil Freemen, Luke Gordon, and Akihiko Sasaki were encouraging of my labors. Most especially, I thank my parents for all their support throughout my debate endeavors.

T.R.H.

Skills

We should be able to enter into other people's ideas and to withdraw from them again; just as we should know how to relinquish our own ideas, and again resume them... It is better to debate a question without settling it, than to settle it without debate.

~ Joseph Joubet, *Thoughts*, 1842

CHAPTER I

Arguing

I've never debated or seen a debate before—I've only argued with my friends and family. What is a debate like?

Most people have never seen a formal debate competition, so their first thoughts are often of emotional arguments they've had with family and friends. If they're interested in the news or the law, most people think next of politics, elections, or courtrooms. This is a good place to begin. As you might guess, debate has a lot more in common with politics or courtrooms than with family disputes! Debate is not about arguing (expressing emotions) but about arguing (discussing ideas).

However, politics and courtrooms are not exactly like competitive debate. I would call politics and courtrooms "democratic" debating: the purpose of the speakers is to influence a collective decision with real consequences. Court decisions and government policies change lives. Because of this, politicians and lawyers tend to believe in what they are fighting for. There is no outcome to the competitive debating students do. Therefore, it is more similar to another, very different kind of debating. Imagine two scientists discussing when the sun will die out. They are not trying to persuade the public to take action; the sun's lifespan is not going to affect anyone's life for a long time. The scientists only want to discuss ideas in order to find the truth. I would call this "academic" debating. Competitive debating is much more like academic debating than democratic debating. Student debaters are not trying to move anyone to action with their debating; they are merely discussing whose ideas are more reasonable. Of course, debaters do often believe passionately in what they argue, but the purpose of competitive debate is the discussion of ideas, not decision-making.

What do you debate about?

Debaters discuss important questions of politics and philosophy, called **topics**. Debaters indirectly discuss:

> Can ideas be dangerous?
> Can ideas change the world?
> What is moral? What is just?
> What type of government is the best?
> Is it even possible to improve society?
> Does humanity have a bright or dark future?
> Is humanity basically good, evil, or something else?

If these questions seem pointless to you, perhaps it's best for you to put down this book—and possibly burn it—and run away from debate. If, on the other hand, these questions make you curious, then perhaps you have the courage to debate.

The courage to debate?

That's right. Becoming a debater is not a simple one-time change but a continual process requiring courage, perseverance, and reflection. It's easy to never question your own opinions; it's comfortable and safe to never have to admit your beliefs might be wrong. Debaters, on the other hand, are by definition always putting their ideas under scrutiny. Debaters prefer asking questions to answering them.

There are three types of people: those who believe they know the Truth and dislike all questions; those who think there is no such thing as truth and believe questions are pointless; and those who are still out seeking the truth. Debaters are the third type. Which are you going to be? It's a choice you must make for yourself. For me, I would prefer to admit doubt than to profess certainty but be wrong.

When I argue with someone, I say that I'm right and he's wrong. How is that questioning myself?

Of course, during a debate, you speak clearly and without ambivalence against an opponent. It's when you're not debating that you question your own opinions. After a debate, you might realize that there's something to what your opponent said. Or before a debate, you might realize that your opinions don't make a lot of sense when you try to explain them.

Experienced debaters know that there are always two defensible sides, for and against, that create reasonable debate about most topics. If both sides weren't reasonable, why would we be debating a topic? After all, no one is ever going to debate 2+2=4 because its truth is self-evident. Sometimes, when you're really into a debate, there comes a moment when you can see the truth of both sides. It is like suddenly removing scales from your eyes. In that instant, you can actually feel yourself becoming smarter, as if your mind just grew two sizes.

Even average debates are fun and informative with plenty of mental gymnastics, even if they're not always perspective altering or life changing. Disagreement with others is the tool, but the goal is still to enlighten yourself. Debate isn't just some activity that you do in class or at a competition and forget about. The way that you look at the world will be altered because you will have learned how other people—that is, your opponents—look at the world.

What are the rules of a debate?

There is a set topic. There are two sides, represented by two different schools: the **affirmative** side, which speaks in agreement with the topic, and the **negative** side, which disagrees. The most important tradition in competitive debate is switching sides. For one debate, you might be assigned Affirmative, but then might be assigned Negative in the next debate. Even if your personal opinion is for the topic, you still have to argue both for and against the topic. You are judged only on how successfully you argue your assigned side.

There are a few simple, absolute rules—for example, time limits: each side gets equal, uninterrupted speech time. Other than that, there are no rules about what debaters can or can't say.

However, there is a judge who decides which side has made better points and therefore wins. Judges do not interfere with a debate unless some rule has been broken (i.e., they cut off speakers who exceed the time limit) and only make their decision at the end of the debate. The more informed debaters, who have better ideas, almost always win. Being prepared is the key to victory.

You said there are no rules about what debaters can or can't say. But then what's to stop a debater from making something up to win?

The short answer is cheaters might win once in a while, but coaches, debaters, and judges eventually ostracize them from the community. The incentive to use deceptive tactics is checked because good debaters quickly notice them—and trained judges decide which side made the best arguments. Because the goal is to continue to impress judges who reward ethical argumentation, any unethical strategy is very shortsighted indeed. Debate is an intellectual martial art where the best ideas win. Doesn't it show that something is defunct with your idea if you have to lie about it to win?

Ethical debaters make good arguments. But what counts as a good argument? One meaning of argument is a personal dispute: argument as yelling. When we say "argument" in normal conversation, this is what we mean. The other meaning of argument is a reason to believe an idea. Most daily speech is not argumentation. We make jokes, we tell stories, we share secrets, and we give orders—all non-arguments that are not appropriate for debates. Argumentation is the process of reasoning back and forth, thus ethical arguments must be reasonable. The emotional appeal or forcefulness of delivery doesn't improve the quality of reasons—or make up for an absence of reasons at all. This book shows you the techniques of the good debater, but it's more important that you become an ethical debater.

Is there anything else to being an ethical debater?

In an informal discussion with a friend about dinner, you can change your **advocacy** (what you are arguing for) as often as your friend can stand your flip-flopping. At first, you might advocate for pizza, then change your mind and argue for spaghetti, and then switch back to pizza. However, your advocacy can never change during a debate. If it were acceptable to change it during a debate, then the last debater to speak would always win—he or she could say or argue whatever was necessary to persuade the judge. Therefore, the rule is simple:

> Once you say it, you're stuck with it.

Of course, you can (and have to) fine-tune the details of what you are advocating. For example, your advocacy might be that the U.S. spends too much on the military. To support this, you could give facts that show how much more money the U.S. spends on the military than any other nation. Later on, you decide that you want to provide additional facts to show the U.S. spends more on the military than it does on foreign aid for humanitarian goals. Has your basic advocacy changed? No. You're advocating that the U.S. spends too much on the military either way; all you've changed is the facts you are using to support that. The rule says that you can't retract facts (withdraw them from the judge's consideration), but you can always provide new ones.

What if there are no ethical arguments for my assigned side?

You might agree with the topic so strongly that it seems impossible to refute it, but don't confuse agreement with an argument with its debatability. Debate topics involve all sorts of current events—political elections, court decisions, social trends, even school policies—that are then connected to broad political, social, and philosophical questions. Topics are designed to have two sides to them. As you learn more about a topic, you will always find arguments on both sides.

Right now, thousands of students across the country are preparing for the very topic on which you will debate them. Even on one given topic, no two debates are ever the same because each debater approaches the same topic with different ideas. Competition is one of the best ways to learn new ideas and test out your own ideas. In fact, you will become knowledgeable about quite a lot of subjects in the process of becoming prepared for your debates.

While you need to be prepared, you also must be flexible. Debate will teach you how to think quickly on your feet and expose you to new ideas you have not yet dreamed of. I guarantee that debate is the most intellectually stimulating, fun activity you will ever do.

Is there a rule of thumb that will help me know what arguments are good before I use them during competition?

It's difficult to specify exactly what should count as a good argument. Many arguments appear to be reasonable at first but seem less and less so the more you think about them. The best way to understand argumentation is by an analogy to science. What is the difference between a scientific theory and a non-scientific one, such as a religious theory? The difference is that the scientific theory can be tested with an experiment. Scientists have an idea—a hypothesis—and then design experiments to test it to see if it's true. With a non-scientific theory, such as a religious theory, it is impossible to set up an experiment to disprove it. For example, how would you set up an experiment to test the existence of God? Scientists throw up their hands and say, "We can't design such an experiment, so we make no theories about God. It's a matter of religious belief, not science."

This is much like the difference between good arguments and bad or non-arguments. An argument is a statement that your opponent can contest in a meaningful way; it is debatable. For example, *Thousands of people are hurt by globalization* is an argument because someone could challenge whether this is factually true or not. Non-arguments against globalization could include: *I hate Nike* because your opponent can't refute your personal preference; *A secret cabal of extraterrestrials runs every company in the world* because your opponent can't refute your unfounded conspiracy theory; *You would understand if you'd been to Africa like me* because your opponent can't refute your experiences. These are not arguments at all but merely your opinions. They are simply impossible to debate; they are debate-enders.

If you would like to know more about the distinction between debatable and non-debatable statements, try reading Karl Popper's *Conjectures and Refutations* (1963). It's fairly advanced philosophy, but it's also written in an accessible style.

How can I become a good debater?

The path to becoming a good debater—which skills you learn best or most easily, which you have to practice at—is unique for each person. Even so, your path doesn't have to be solitary. If something confuses you, ask your teacher or a more experienced debater to explain it. We all learn piecemeal: if an idea isn't making sense right away, don't panic! You will find everything eventually makes sense; all your skills will come together—just perhaps not when you expect them to. To become a good debater, treat learning as a never-ending process, not as a goal to be reached as quickly as possible.

Never accept any answer as final, including mine. No one has a monopoly on the truth. That's why I want to caution you against even this book: <u>never</u> quote it, <u>never</u> memorize it, and <u>never</u> believe anything in it unless you think things through for yourself. In fact, if anyone ever quotes this book at you, here is your response:

> Everything in *The "How to" of Debate* is wrong.

Never ask yourself: "Is this the correct answer?" Instead ask: "Does this make sense to me?" You must find your own reasonable answers. Question everything and assume nothing.

At this point, you probably still have a lot of unanswered questions about debate, like:

How do I debate?
What is a debate competition like?
Will I have a partner, or will I be by myself?
What kind of help will I receive from my coach?
What happens if I blank when I stand up to speak?

The first section of this book answers these questions and describes the five skills every debater must acquire: (1) being an ethical advocate (this chapter), (2) listening and note taking, (3) speaking, (4) researching, and (5) briefing. The skills are straightforward, but it takes time and practice to become a master of them. The second section of this book covers debating the Affirmative. The third section covers debating the Negative. The final section of this book, *Rhetoric*, covers the specifics of competition.

Review questions:

1. Compare and contrast competitive, interscholastic debating to democratic debating.

2. Compare and contrast competitive, interscholastic debating to academic debating.

3. Define "topic," "affirmative," and "negative."

4. Explain how to debate ethically in terms of arguments and advocacy. Give counterexamples of a debater doing something unethical.

5. Give three examples of debatable arguments and three examples of non-arguments.

6. Why do I want you to never quote this book?

Milestone:

You, your teammates, and your coach should have had a discussion about how to play the game of debate fairly. At this point, you should understand what it means to be an ethical debater, and I hope your coach will ask you to sign an ethics pledge.

CHAPTER 2

Flowing

I don't understand why we are talking about note taking first. It seems like a boring thing to have to talk about. Shouldn't speaking or even reasoning be first? Why is note taking so important?

A debate is not a static thing; instead, there is a constant, fluid back-and-forth flow. Each side in a debate states its advocacy clearly but then immediately and continually must respond to opponent challenges. Presenting your ideas effectively is only part of the equation; adapting is crucial. If you think of your advocacy in a debate as static, then you're likely to find a debate very confusing. If you see that your advocacy needs continual fine-tuning, then you're more likely to be flexible, be adaptable, and do well. We start with the concept of flow because it's so important to understanding the game of debate.

Given how rapidly a debate evolves, listening carefully to your opponent and taking notes is necessary to keep up. Debates are simply too complex to remember. Just think of how many arguments you and your opponent could make in one debate: up to 5,000-7,000 words—per side. Without good notes, you could never possibly follow a full-length debate. Flowing is the skill of listening and note taking. We call these notes the flow of the debate, or simply, the **flow**. Each person watching or participating in a debate should have his or her own flow. Even the judge has a flow.

So a flow is a record of the debate?

Yes, but a flow is far more than a mere record; the flow affects how the debaters speak. The fact that a judge flows changes how you must present your arguments, how you challenge your opponents' reasons, and even what ideas you choose to advocate compared to how you might do all of these things during an informal debate where no one took any notes. Because notes are being taken, it means that you must be more accurate, that you can use more facts, and that you can never get away with altering your basic advocacy. In a way, the flow is like a chessboard on which you and your opponent move your arguments about like chess pieces. The flow is the game board of debate. I would even go so far as to say that the flow is the debate; I like to think of speaking as "flowing aloud," but some people believe this is going too far.

Good flows are a crucial first step for good reasoning and good speaking. First, if you have a good flow, it ensures that you can **clash** (clearly and directly refute) with your opponent's arguments. Good debates always have clash. The opposite situation— where your arguments and your opponent's arguments pass like ships in the night—is unpleasant for everyone, and is useless for testing ideas, like what passes for debate on talk radio. Second, a good flow can keep you from accidentally forgetting to talk about arguments. If your opponent makes an argument, you must answer it in your next speech, or else you've forfeited the right to refute it. You have **conceded** that it is true by doing nothing. In a court of law, this is known as stipulation. Some debaters even try **spreading:** presenting so many arguments that they force their opponents to concede something by default. Of course, you can choose to concede an argument for a strategic purpose—maybe the argument isn't even worth responding to—but that should be a conscious decision, not one that happens because of sloppy flowing. On the other side, if an opponent concedes your argument, then you should point it out!

If I miss my opponents' argument, then I'm going to lose?

Yes. In sports, a goal still counts, even if the goalie was momentarily districted. The same is true in debate. All that matters is what you actually say, not what you intended to say. Therefore, good debaters must be good at flowing. The primary characteristic of debaters who are good at flowing is that they listen carefully. Listening is about understanding, not just hearing. If you don't understand what someone is saying, how can you refute them? Too often, we hear what we want to hear, not what the other person is actually saying. One key barrier to listening is mental laziness. We hear a few words of an idea and then fill in the rest for ourselves. The problem is that most people express themselves with lots of twists, and the first words might not be indicative of where they finish. Many debaters are guilty of a mistake known as defensive listening: they begin to write their response before they fully understand their opponent's argument. Of course, the usual outcome is that they refute an argument that wasn't made and ignore the one that was made—a needless concession. Listening to an idea all the way through, or at least until you're absolutely certain, is important.

The larger barriers to careful listening are our natural mental filters. For example, consider this sentence: "Last January, I went to the beach to swim a lot." This might confuse people who live in the northern hemisphere for a minute, but those in the southern hemisphere understood it right away. Northerners know January to be cold and imagine the swimmer in icy waters, whereas Southerners know that January is quite warm and imagine a beautiful month of surf and sun. The point is that all listeners have mental filters: we make and use assumptions about the way the world works. Getting beyond your assumptions is the second hurdle to listening. Unless you can put your filters on pause, your flow may not accurately reflect your debate. If this happens, your flow will be a detriment rather than an asset in your debate. The only way to effectively adapt during a debate is to recognize your real strengths and weaknesses in a debate, rather than hearing what you want to hear.

I've been taking notes in every class since the fourth grade. Isn't flowing just like regular note taking?

For goodness' sake, no! Flowing is a special kind of note taking. In a classroom, only one person is speaking: the teacher. You write down the important points in the order that the speaker (teacher) makes them. In debate, there are two sides speaking, with multiple speeches, and the key points might be in a different order in each speech because each side organizes its thinking differently, each talking about the arguments it is trying to use to win. Don't think of a flow as simple transcript. Think of a flow as a spreadsheet or table, like so:

1st Aff Speech	1st Neg Speech	2nd Aff Speech	Etc.
Argument 1	Challenge A to arg. 1	Response to challenge A	...
	Challenge B to arg. 1	Response to challenge B	
Argument 2	Challenge C to arg. 2	Response to challenges C & D	...
	Challenge D to arg. 2		
	Challenge E to arg. 2	Response to challenge E	
Argument 3	Challenge G to arg. 3	Response to challenge G	...

This row-and-column format is the essential difference between a flow and regular notes. The columns represent each speech. The rows track each argument through its initial presentation, to challenges, then responses, and so forth. When determining whether an argument stands or falls, a judge quickly scans the row to see the development of the argument throughout the debate. If your opponent speaks out of order and leads off with his response to challenge E before jumping to his response to challenge B, well, you had better flow the arguments in the right places in the chart. The judge will.

Please don't think that you have to write out a perfect flow on your first try! Flowing is a skill that needs constant practice. Even expert debaters and coaches still need to practice. The best way to practice is by watching and flowing other people's debates. On the other hand, watching a debate without flowing is nearly useless. The second best way is to flow TV or radio news. Each news story is like an argument, and you can list all the important facts as though they were supporting points. Plus, this will make you more informed about current events, which is always good for debaters!

There's a lot coming at me while I try to flow. I just don't write fast enough. Are there any special techniques to getting everything?

Good question. One trick to flowing is that you only need to write down arguments. This is why listening is vital to flowing. Don't write your opponent's speech out word-for-word on your flow. It's a waste of time and effort. If your opponent blathers on for several minutes, you don't need to write down anything at all. Beware, though: within a poor speech, there is often a kernel of a good argument. You have to listen carefully to tease out the good arguments from a windbag. Good listening is about separating the arguments from the non-arguments.

A second trick to flowing is to write less. The purpose of a flow is to remind you of arguments that either you or your opponent made in the debate. You don't need to write out every little detail, and you won't be able to keep up if you do. Usually, you only need a word or two to remind you of a whole argument. And where possible, use abbreviations.

A third trick is to flow your own arguments in one color of ink, and your opponents' arguments in another color. When you scan the flow, you can quickly identify what you need to refute and you won't get caught up refuting your own points. Furthermore, flowing in two ink colors allows you to honestly assess your strengths and weaknesses. Comparing ink can be a pretty good visual clue of how well you're doing on different arguments in the debate. I would also recommend putting stars, boxes, circles, or some other marks around key arguments (yours and your opponents') for easy reference.

Finally, I recommend spreading your flow over several pieces of paper. Any debate is actually made up of several sub-debates. For example, in a debate about fighting terrorism, *Fighting terrorism is expensive* might be one sub-debate, and *Terrorism is unlikely nowadays* might be another. All these sub-debates are relevant to the overall debate topic but are distinct from each other. I recommend using a new piece of paper for each one. It allows you to easily reorganize: if you want to talk about cost first, put that piece of paper on top. For one debate, I might spread my flow out over twelve pieces of paper, although it's not usually that many. Separate pieces of paper help keep all the component parts distinct.

On the next page, there's a sample flow from a fictitious debate. It is an ideal flow, neat and typed (thanks to Owen Zahorcak). Obviously, real flows seldom look as clean. As you're learning how to flow, try your best to write down all the arguments you can catch; worry about neatness when you have a little experience.

1st Neg speech	2nd Aff speech	2nd Neg speech	3rd Aff speech	3rd Neg speech
	1. Who cares? <u>SS = low now</u> Terry '05 (b/c ugly building)	1. Johnson is right, not Terry -- SS is low (Johnson is better b/c sports-specific)	1. B-ball win = one-time thing 2. Building always ugly	They concede SS high now, even if temporary only a risk that of reducing it b4 big game
A. Students uncrtn about new prncpl <u>Smith '05</u>				
	2. SS low now b/c 1st string quarterback injured	1. 2nd string QB still good - will win game ⟶		They also conc we'll win the game with 2nd QB
B. <u>SS = high now</u> Johnson '05 (b/c b-ball win)		1. Yes they do I saw one yesterday		
	3. Articles irrel b/c Football players Ø read paper	2. Irrel - fans do, & SS <u>k</u> to cheering		
		3. <u>Cheering decides games</u> Lombardi '67	1. Ø mean he's an expert, I'm paid to mow the lawn + I'm bad at it	
C. Critical articles ↓SS <u>Reynolds '03</u> (auth = principal)	4. Unreliable source: Reynolds = principal, so he's self-interested	1. Principals know best -- monitor SS for a living	2. Auth Ø credible "Don't make fun of me" = whining	
			1. Teenagers still cynical, annoying	1. Aff's story does make sense - anti-admin articles only ↓ SS
D. ↓ SS ⟶ to ↓ football team confid & loss <u>homecoming game</u> George '04	5. Critical articles ↑ happiness w/ <u>cynical teenagers</u> Roberts '97	1. Happiness ≠ SS, only Reynolds is spec. to SS	2. Arg = silly Football fans SS is same as their happiness	2. Even if critical articles make kids smirk, not ↑ SS
				3. Aff can only incr introspection about school quality - only a risk of ↓SS
	6. Academic freedom more impt than football	1. Homecoming game super impt b/c it's a soc ev		

It looks cool but confusing. What is the debate about? Why is there no first affirmative speech?

The topic here is: *Highland School should permit articles critical of its administration to be published in its school newspaper.* This is only one piece of flow paper from the debate. This is a flow of a negative attack: *Allowing such articles in the school newspaper would harm school spirit, leading to a homecoming game loss.* This flow starts with a negative speech because this is an attack raised by the Negative. There are only five speeches flowed, one in each column, because this sub-debate ended after the third negative speech.

What are all those abbreviations? Do I have to memorize a set of them?

You can invent any abbreviations you want, as long you can remember them (make sure your partner also knows them!). There are several techniques to develop good abbreviations. In this example, some abbreviations use initials (*SS* for school spirit), some eliminate vowels (like *prncpl* for principal), some use symbols (*Ø* for not, *→* for leads to), some foreshorten (*irrel, b/c, b4,* etc.). Think of it like text messaging: get the most meaning possible for the least typing.

What are all the lines and numbers about?

The stair-step lines (the big *S*s between columns) keep track of which arguments respond to which. As you can see, some rows get too crowded, and you may have to bump things around to make them fit. It's just a way to make efficient use of space on the piece of paper. You either need to keep the rows of argumentation lined up or use the stair-step lines.

When you speak, make sure you make it clear which argument you are talking about. That is, always number your own arguments or refer to your opponent's argument by name and number. This technique is known as **line-by-line** debating, answering your opponent's key arguments in an organized, clear, systematic way. This makes it easier to flow you and makes your speech clearer. Everyone needs to see how the arguments line up against each other. Chapter 3 explains in detail how to do line-by-line debating.

What is the circle about? The arrow?

That's something that speakers sometimes do to remind themselves to point out that an opponent conceded something. If you look carefully at the flow, you'll see that the Negative doesn't respond to everything—only the important things. You don't have to answer every argument, but you do need to **cover** (speak about) all the important ones. Circles, stars, or boxes are quick visual clues for a speaker to remember what's important to cover.

Why are there all the names and dates?

These arguments are direct quotations from experts, books, journals, newspapers, or websites. Most competitions allow direct quotations. Often, a debater will make an argument, and to support it, read a relevant quotation from an expert, including, of course, the author's last name and the year of publication. You don't need to write out the whole quotation on your flow, which would be impossible. You only flow the argument that the debater is making and the author and year of the quotation.

Underneath this, I like to flow any comments I have about the quality of the quotation. Does it seem to support the argument? Why should your opponent's expert quotations stand unchallenged? Knock holes wherever possible.

Can I use a computer to flow a debate?

If you can't seem to get the knack of it on paper, you might try using a computer spreadsheet, such as Excel, Apache OpenOffice (free), LibreOffice (free), or an offline Google doc spreadsheet (free). However, some debate competitions do not yet allow debaters to use computers during debates, so check the rules first. Furthermore, using a computer spreadsheet for flowing can be harder to manage than using paper. Beginners ought to flow on paper for simplicity.

Review questions:

1. Explain why it is vital for everyone in a debate to flow.

2. Why is flowing not like taking class notes?

3. Define "clash," "concede," "spread," and "cover."

4. What are some of the barriers to listening? How do you remove these barriers?

5. What is line-by-line debating? What flowing techniques will help you do good line-by-line debating?

6. What flowing techniques help you flow more quickly?

Milestone:

You should have watched and flowed several debates of beginners and intermediates already. Take time to go back and polish these flows: rewrite them using all the techniques we've discussed to make the flows simple and clear (abbreviations, colors, stair-step lines, etc.). Now it is time to try flowing some experienced debaters!

CHAPTER 3

Speaking

I watched some experienced debaters. Now I'm intimidated! They're amazing speakers: they don't stumble, they make intelligent points, and they're fast. How in the world can I possibly beat them?

When beginning debaters see advanced debaters, their first reaction is often shock. The advanced debaters speak so confidently, so fluidly, and so quickly that some beginners are intimidated right out of debate. Relax. Of course advanced debaters speak well! They've had lots of practice. Do you watch Stephen Curry and think, "Wow, why should I bother playing basketball?" No. It's the same with speaking. If you practice, then in time, you too can speak that well.

The most obvious skill of advanced debaters is their speaking speed. A normal conversational speaking speed is 150 words per minute (wpm). When excited, we might jump up to 200 wpm. Some debaters, on the other hand, can get above 300 wpm. Why do they need to speak so quickly? In debate, unlike in normal conversation, there are time limits. As you can figure, debaters speaking at 300 wpm can fit in twice as many words—thus, twice as many arguments—as someone plodding along at 150 wpm. That's the obvious advantage to speaking quickly. However, there are downsides. Some debaters speak more quickly than their judges can flow. This is dumb. Getting in more arguments is useless if the judge can't flow them. Furthermore, the faster you try to go, the more likely you are to stumble or to be unclear. All these mistakes use up time, which leads to the paradox of speed speaking:

> You are often faster when you go slower.

Don't believe me? Test it for yourself. Read an article as fast as you possibly can. How many words per minute did you achieve? Now try it reading the same article as fast <u>as is comfortable</u> for you. How many words per minute was that? Every debater has a "sweet spot," a point of maximum clarity and words per minute. The trick is that your sweet spot is not the maximum speed at which you can shovel words out your mouth, but at about 80–90% of that.

If I speak at 80% of my top speed, there is just no way I could speak as quickly as the experienced debaters. What should I do?

Don't sweat it. As you become prepared—become familiar with your arguments—your speed naturally increases. As you become more experienced, your speed naturally increases. You can also work to improve your clarity and speed with speaking drills. The goal is to be clear rather than to be fast! The best way to improve your speaking is to do about five minutes of drills per day, each and every day. Think of them as musical scales or as stretches, pushing your envelope gradually; don't adopt a "no pain, no gain" mindset. Five minutes is plenty of time; what is crucial is your consistency in doing them every day.

One recommendation for any drill is to use or make a lectern. This will enable you to have maximum realism while practicing. Here are the ten best drills I have run across. All of these drills (except the tenth) assume reading from something like a newspaper or book. It can help to practice from articles on your current debate topic.

1. <u>Backwards drill</u>: Backwards word-for-word quotations read. Do can you things effective most the of one is this, true but, strange. Eyes your follow to mouth your train helps it. Don't reprint the quotation backwards; it's all about retraining your eyes to move in a different way across the page.

2. Vowel drill: Read -A- quotations -A- and -A- insert -A- a -A- vowel -A- in -A- between -A- every -A- word. This is also known as the Taking-the-A-train drill. Other vowels like "O" work equally well. This trains your eyes to keep pace with your mouth.

3. Speed drill: Begin reading very slowly, at a normal speaking speed. Very gradually, increase the speed until you're going as fast as you can. Then, slow down. Repeat this cycle several times to train yourself to control your speed, neither too fast nor too slow.

4. Read-a-line-and-breathe drill: Try to read one full line of text from the left margin to the right margin without stopping. Then, when you get to the end of the line, pause and take a nice, deep breath. Repeat until you pass out. The point of this drill is training your eyes to read one whole line of text at one whack.

5. Pen drill: Read with a pen in your mouth and make yourself intelligible. This always produces lots of spit, so wear a bib. Most people are physically lazy speakers, and the pen forces you to work harder.

6. Enunciation drill: O-ver pro-nounce ev-ery sin-gle syl-la-ble while rea-ding. This serves the same purpose as the pen drill, but at least you don't look like a horse with a bit in its mouth.

7. Emphasis drill: Imagine that you are a terrible actor, and vary your inflection, pitch, and volume absurdly. Monotony is a constant danger in debating, so cheese it up.

8. Diaphragm drill: Read while holding a chair up; hold it with your arms as horizontal as you can! It strengthens your chest muscles and lungs. On a related note, standing up without slouching when speaking is best for your lungs. Sitting to speak unnecessarily puts pressure on your diaphragm, with greater effort for worse results.

9. Rapping drill: Speak in rhythm to music. This is surprisingly effective as well as lots of fun. Seriously. I've seen it work miracles. Our natural lack of rhythm causes us to stumble and

stutter, but with background music providing a rhythm, we
speak smoothly. Try it!

10. <u>Tongue twister drill</u>: (This is the only one that isn't reading
    from a book or newspaper.) Try saying tongue twisters as fast
    you can. "Red leather, yellow leather" is particularly chal-
    lenging, or try "Toy boat." I also recommend, "Rubber baby
    buggy bumpers."

The best way to approach your drills is to simply cycle through
them and do a different drill each night. The ones you don't like
doing will be those drills that will help you the most. If you think
of other drills, please feel free to add them to your own personal
repertoire.

Another tip: if you ever do run out of air while speaking, try
resting your hands on the small of your back. It helps aid deep
breathing.

*When I watched a debate, I didn't really follow it. The two sides
kept going back and forth, but how is a debate organized?*

To follow the thrusts (claims) and parries (refutations) of each
speaker, you need to understand how each speech is important to
the entire debate **round**, that is, one debate from beginning to end.

There are three types of speech in any debate—constructives,
rebuttals, and cross-examinations—and each has a few special
limits on the content. **Constructives** are for both sides to state
their basic advocacy and thus begin debates. **Rebuttals** are for
summarizing and tweaking your arguments and responding to an
opponent's challenges. No new arguments are allowed in rebuttals. The test of novelty is whether a debater is merely making an
idea stronger (acceptable) or is starting to argue an entirely new
idea (unacceptable). **Cross-examinations** are question-and-answer
periods between one of the debaters and an opponent. Let's look
at when each speech is used.

Opening constructives

The Affirmative sets forth its advocacy. The only job of the
Affirmative by the end of the debate is to win its original points,
so the Affirmative plays defense during a debate. Therefore, you

never want to wing the first affirmative constructive speech. You want to have your speech thoroughly planned because your advocacy can't be changed in any major way.

The only job of the Negative is to attack the Affirmative as presented. For this reason, the first negative constructive speech must be adapted to each and every Affirmative in slightly different ways. The Negative can predict and thus prepare many of its attacks in advance, but there are always last minute tweaks. The first negative constructive speech is modular, where a few appropriate attacks are selected from dozens the Negative has prewritten on the topic.

Middle speeches

Middle speeches include both constructives and rebuttals, and while the limits on new content are different, the purpose is the same. The Affirmative responds to the negative attacks and further develops its advocacy. The Affirmative can provide new arguments to defend its advocacy, but something has gone wrong if the Affirmative has to abandon its old arguments. The Negative can launch new lines of attack and develop its original lines of attack from its first constructive. In the middle speeches, good line-by-line debating is vital. You want to creatively reshape the arguments that you have and get rid of the arguments that aren't working. At this point, each side is developing the complexity of its arguments but also narrowing down the number of arguments it's making.

Concluding rebuttals

The final rebuttals are very distinct. It's best to be narrow but deep, as opposed to wide but shallow, in the final rebuttals. Line-by-line debating is de-emphasized. Instead, you spend more time presenting a holistic picture of the debate and generally being persuasive. The Affirmative is summarizing, proving that its advocacy has survived all of the negative attacks. The final negative rebuttal is also a speech of summary, but it is distinct in that the Negative is still on the attack. Rather than summarize all of its attacks, the Negative is wise to emphasize only one or two, but summarize all the reasons why these attacks are fatal. One serious flaw is enough of a reason by itself for the judge to vote for the Negative, against the Affirmative.

What about the cross-examinations? Are there rules?

In most debates, the cross-examinations are formal periods with defined time limits mixed in throughout the debate. There are a few goals when you're the cross-examiner and a few goals when you're the cross-examined. On either side of the equation, be polite. Because you may be focused on the outcome of the debate, it's easy to become too intense, or the questions may make you defensive. On the other hand, you don't want to be too passive. It's best to strike a balance: you need to be direct with your questions and answers without being rude or taking it personally, and even if your opponent is rude, don't take it as an excuse for losing your cool.

But what is the point of cross-examination?

You can use cross-examination to achieve three different goals: get more information, set up your opponent, and make key arguments. First, you may need to learn about your opponent's arguments. What exactly is he saying? What was her third argument? You can tear into your opponent's supporting facts—it's best to do this in cross-examination, rather than waste your precious speech time. What do his quotations support, and what do they not support? Make those quotations look weak, and then give better quotations in your speech.

Second, cross-examination gives you the opportunity to trick your opponent. Usually, the judge <u>doesn't flow</u> cross-examination, but you can use it to establish an argument in the judge's mind before you make it in your next speech. You can ask hard questions; you can lay traps or work your opponent into a corner; or you can try to get your opponent to concede something. However, be careful! Never ask a question as a trap if you don't already know the answer to it. These rough tactics could blow up in your face if your opponent is too clever, so use the tactics with a lot of restraint and caution.

However, the best use of cross-examination is neither asking what arguments your opponent made, nor trying to trick your opponent into making mistakes. The best use of cross-examination is as a special arena for very subtle argumentation. Because your opponent is forced to respond, you can quickly go back and forth several times, past the surface of the idea to the real reasons behind it. You can ask your opponent to explain his or her arguments by asking, "What would I need to do to disprove your argument?" An honest debater <u>must</u> explain refutations that you might want to consider. For example, your opponent might say something like, "Well, you could argue A or maybe B, although I think they're both bad arguments." This debater honestly answered the question but stayed consistent to her position.

When you're the one being cross-examined, be honest and provide the most thorough answers that you can. Feigning ignorance looks bad. However, if you genuinely don't know, then don't be afraid to admit it—possibly the question makes no sense. Obviously, don't walk right into traps. It's best to call your opponent out: "Well, if you're trying to trick me into saying A, it won't work because..." If your opponent throws you a softball question, then swing away: when he gives you free rein and won't cut you off, then keep speaking. It's free speech time for you!

The experienced debaters were also really good at making their points. I tend to ramble on before I get to my point. How can I practice that?

Well, you practice delivery with drills, but practicing content is trickier. You become more concise (the opposite of rambling) the more experienced you are. It is especially important that you know your material well. If you are well prepared, you aren't going to ramble. If you aren't familiar with your arguments, of course you ramble.

Generally, the problem most beginners have is that debate speaking is not like normal conversation. Most normal conversation is talking to someone who's probably half-listening—so you repeat yourself a lot. In debate, you're talking to a judge and opponents who are furiously taking notes. They are not at all like listeners thinking about lunch while you talk. A judge or opponent does not need repetition because it is flowed the first time. Also remember that there is a time limit in debate: you must deliver your speech within its time limit, or you will be cut off. It is irrelevant to the judge if you had many good arguments but ran out of time, and your opponent will be happy if you make this mistake.

That is why you need to re-orient yourself when you debate: you're not speaking to your opponents, or even to the judge. Instead, you're speaking to the judge's flow, moving arguments around on the debate chessboard. As a speaker, your aim is to have the most effect on the judge's flow using the least speech time. This is how judo works—using little motions to throw an opponent around. Or think of headlines. Newspapers have little space to tell you what the story is about but still need to get their point across. Headlines are efficient and economical.

That is why the most important speaking skill in debate is **word economy**: making your arguments in the fewest words necessary. Word economy is like oral abbreviations because debate is not about flowery eloquence, only your arguments. A friend and I used to have contests where we tried to win informal debates with the fewest words possible. He always beat me because most of his arguments were one or two words long! Obviously this is extreme, but it can be done. These are skills that you can improve with practice debates. Everyone can double his word economy, but no one can double her speed. Good word economy beats raw speed every time: quality trumps quantity. This is why experienced debaters have to be able to deliver a well-organized speech, covering all the important arguments point-by-point without repetition. Word economy is another reason why good line-by-line debating is so important.

Is that why the experienced debaters sounded like they were speaking in code, with all these numbers and weird phrases?

Yes. There are eight techniques that debaters use during line-by-line debating. These techniques are like speaking in outline form: having all your arguments organized clearly and subordinating less important points. Or you can think of it as "speaking in flow" as I do. They can sound a little unnatural, but using them is essential. It is about being systematic in covering all the key points.

1. Roadmaps: Before you begin your speech, you'll need to give a brief roadmap, basically telling everyone how to order the different pieces of flow paper. No one needs a preview of your arguments, merely their order: "First, I'm going to talk about flow A, then I'll move on to flow B, and finish with C." Providing the judge a roadmap should not count against your speech time. You should roadmap before every speech except the first speech.

2. Signposts: Signposting is a roadmap during your speech. You should tell everyone when you've moved from one piece of flow paper to another: "Now I'm finished talking about flow A, and I'm moving on to flow B."

3. Numbers: Always number your own arguments, and refer to your opponent's arguments by number: "On my opponent's 2nd argument, my answer is..." It can't be overstated how helpful this is to everyone in the debate. Even if you get the numbers wrong, it's still helpful because you're probably approximately right.

4. Grouping: If your opponent repeats the same argument several times in a row, you need to group them and answer them once. Simply say, "Group my opponent's 2nd, 3rd, and 4th arguments—they are all the same," before giving your answers one time.

5. Cross-applications: If your opponent repeats the same argument non-consecutively, you can cross-apply your refutations. You answer the argument for the first time in your normal way. When you get to the argument the second time, you say, "Cross-apply my answers from his 3rd argument here."

6. Extensions: If your opponent concedes your argument, you need to make sure that you point it out, or extend the argument. You say: "Extend my 3rd argument. He dropped it, and therefore conceded it." Then explain the importance of the argument to the debate.

7. Concessions: For strategic reasons, you often need to concede some arguments to your opponent. Only concede what can't hurt you: "I concede her 3rd argument; however, she overstates its importance..." Beginning debaters are rarely willing to let go of any arguments. It is understandable, but successful debaters don't win every argument—they win the ones that matter the most.

8. Overviews: You need to provide a brief summary in each speech. Don't use these overviews to make arguments—that's what you should do on the line-by-line. Use your overviews to be persuasive and to state the importance of your arguments.

In the final minute of your final speech, provide a final summary for the entire debate.

Review questions:

1. Why is trying to speak too quickly actually counterproductive?

2. Define "round," "constructive," "rebuttal," and also "cross-examination."

3. What is the goal for each side in its opening constructive? in the middle speeches? in its concluding rebuttal?

4. What are the three goals of cross-examination? Discuss which goal is the most important.

5. Why is word economy so important?

6. Explain how to use each of the eight speaking techniques for giving word economical, line-by-line speeches.

Milestone:

At this point, you should be participating in practice rounds against other beginning debaters. On the first day, start with just one cross-examination. On the next day, do a cross-examination and a response speech. On the third day, do a cross-examination, a response speech, and then the next cross-examination. Work up until you are doing full practice rounds. Work on your word economy; use the eight speaking techniques to do line-by-line debating! Also, you should be doing practice cross-examinations to work on your questioning techniques.

To be honest, research seems boring. Plus I got into debate because everyone always says I have a lot of opinions. Can't I just get by with whatever I already know?

Absolutely not! Where to begin? First of all, you might know a lot—compared to non-debaters or beginners—but you'll find that debaters know a lot more about a topic than the average person. If you don't do research, your opponent is going to wallop you with superior arguments. Believe me, it is not much fun speaking when you, your opponent, <u>and</u> the judge know that you have no idea what you're talking about. Rounds are won or lost in the library. Second, remember that most debate rules allow direct quotations, so you can quote experts directly. Research helps you come up with all that content you need to fill your speeches, and doing it well will give you the confidence that your opinions are backed by facts. One of the best feelings in the world is realizing that a scholar with two PhDs, who has spent her life researching the topic, came to the same conclusions that you've already come to, and besides, quotations from respected scholars are more credible than your mere assertions, anyway.

I could go on with a lot more reasons for doing research, but I think I know your root objection: research doesn't seem very creative. However, this isn't strictly true. Really smart people might have already published their thoughts about your topic, but you have to figure out you will use what they've said. You can't simply restate someone else's idea; you have to figure out how to use what they wrote to support your own arguments. Researching how you can support your own arguments with expert quotations requires active thinking and can be as much or even more fun than delivering that quotation in a round. Nothing feels better than finding an awesome quotation that will render your next opponent speechless.

However, please don't ever believe that research lifts your burden of arguing. The quotations you find are only tools to help you make arguments. Even with good research, it is your explanation of the argument that is crucial; research merely provides support for the argument. For example, you might read a quotation that contains complicated technical terms. If you can't basically explain what it all means, then you probably shouldn't quote it. As another example, you might read a quotation that uses statistical information. Statistics can be very useful, but you need to have some familiarity with how the information was gathered and who calculated it. What if it turns out that the statistics were gathered by a really biased source that lied or distorted the information? What happens if your opponent knows that but you don't? It won't be a fun round.

So how do I find these awesome quotations?

Good quotations are really a by-product of researching thoroughly. If you learn about your topic in general, then you inevitably find them. But before you start looking for authors who support your advocacy, you need to get a sense of the lay of the land. What are people saying about your topic? You have to start with an open mind at this point. Cast a wide net. At first, hang on to any articles that seem interesting—even if you are not sure they're useful.

At this stage of the research process, your only product is what is known as a **literature review** of the topic. A literature review can be written down as a concept map or a brief essay, or your teacher may just ask you to give it as an oral presentation to other students. The important part is that a literature review describes the main viewpoints of authors writing about a topic. Pay attention to how experts refute each other—how does author A respond to author B's idea? However, you will discover that all sides agree on certain issues. For example, everyone agrees that the AIDS epidemic in Africa is out of control. The debate is really about how to respond to this crisis, and this is exactly the kind of information you want to gain for your literature review. Furthermore, seek out unusual viewpoints; no one should be able to blindside you in a debate with an argument you've never heard of. Reviewing the literature gives you an incredibly confident feeling during your debates, knowing no one can catch you off-guard.

Where do I research?

The Internet is a good place to start researching. Wikipedia has good introductory information about many debate topics and, most important, has external links to other sources, including websites and books. However, Wikipedia has a unique problem: because an article has no author and no fixed form, you can't quote it in a debate round. I'm sure you know that, in general, you can't trust everything on the Internet. It is a mixed bag: some excellent sources, a lot of mediocre sites, and some that are downright crazy. Use the Internet with caution—always think about whether you've found a credible source. Despite all these caveats, the Internet is the best way to start your research.

The next step is to hit the electronic databases. These computerized databases are specialized collections of newspapers, magazines, and most important, academic journals. You can search through a database by typing in keywords, and then print or download an electronic copy (usually in html or PDF) of each article you find. Some high schools and public libraries have access to a few databases, but the main subscribers are college libraries. They often subscribe to dozens of specialized databases. The most famous database is Lexis-Nexis, which has news and law reviews. Law reviews are especially full of good articles! Two other useful databases are WorldCat and ArticleFirst, which are comprehensive reference listings for books and articles. If a book is in any college library in the world, WorldCat knows it.

Can I even get in to a college library if I'm not a college student?

Generally, yes. Most colleges have programs to allow people in the community to enter. Just ask the librarians. While you're at it, ask the librarians for help using the catalog to search for books. This is the second reason to go to a good college library. Only college libraries tend to have enough good books about typical debate topics to make it worth your while to check out. Compared to the ease of using the Internet, researching in books can seem slow and inefficient, but books have a wealth of information that isn't available in other formats. Besides, finding good books is not hard. In the Library of Congress catalog system, which most college libraries use, the most useful books for debaters are in the Hs (social science), Js (political science), or Ks (law). Books in each field are numbered by topic. Whenever you find a useful book, look carefully at its neighbors, and you might stumble onto something else good. Scan tables of contents, flip through the index, or read the first few paragraphs in introductions and last few in conclusions of promising books. At this point, your objective is not to read them all—your goal is still merely your literature review.

You should also check to see if the library subscribes to any paper journals it does not receive electronically. Many libraries have several journals in hard copy only. These usually are kept on special shelves or in a current periodicals section. If in doubt, ask a librarian for help finding them. You may think that librarians don't want to be bothered with your research. Nothing could be farther from the truth. Librarians are positively giddy when asked for help.

The third reason to check out the college library (or sometimes the public library) is government documents. Our government produces reams of documents, on all different kinds of topics. This research is often loaded with statistics and data that the government collected. There might be a wealth of specific information or data for your topic. Government documents have their own special cataloging system, the SuDoc number. For these reasons, government documents can be a bit of a pain to research, but they can be worth it.

So I've found an awesome article that supports my advocacy, and I bet no one else has read it. Someone is going to get a big surprise. It felt like I'd already won a debate round when I found it. Now what?

After you complete your literature review, you're ready for the second stage: targeted research. Out of all the different arguments you have found, you decide to focus on one or a few ideas that you want to use in your debates. Luckily, if you have one awe-some article or book, it can lead you to many more. All research is cumulative: authors list all their research, meaning that if you track down your author's sources, you're likely to find additional articles and books making similar arguments. In essence, you're getting a research guide from Professor John Q. Expert. Why rein-vent the wheel when his bibliography is right in front of you? Check the book's or article's bibliography, endnotes, or footnotes. Debaters call this **rabbit trailing**. Your goal is to begin to hit the rabbit trails as soon as you can. Typing keywords in a catalog is a shotgun approach: some hits, a lot of misses. Rabbit trailing is much more targeted. You can also check the Social Sciences Cita-tion Index, which is a record of the other authors who refer to the article you have in hand (i.e., rabbit trailing in reverse). Most good college libraries have the S.S.C.I., maybe on a special com-puter terminal.

Rabbit trailing and the S.S.C.I. turn up the most amazing things. I have sworn that there is not one good book in the library when doing a catalog search, found one good article in the data-bases, then hit the S.S.C.I. and rabbit trails, only to discover that the library was jammed full of books that I could use. All it takes is the key.

At the end of this second stage of more focused research, you will have many articles and books about the particular stance that you want to take. Now you're ready to move onto the third stage.

I've done all this research, I've found all these articles, and I'm still not done? What else is there to do?

The third stage of research is turning the articles you found during the literature review and targeted researching into direct or para-phrased quotations to support your arguments. You couldn't quote even one page from each article you found during one de-bate round. The desire to quote everything is known as "research rapture." Some articles are interesting and informative back-grounders but not quotable. You need to be honest with yourself about the quality of the articles you've found. Which parts of this article are worth quoting? Is it a commonly held view, or if not, are you comfortable going out on a limb with it? Is this author credible enough to quote? If you answer "no" to any of these questions, then you better keep looking. If you don't do this gut-check before leaving the library, your opponents will do it for you during a round. Talk to people on your team if in doubt. There are three qualities of good quotations: timeliness, credibility, and validity.

The timeliness is the most straightforward quality. Most quotations should be from the last 2-3 years. Of course, for some arguments, such as definitions or philosophical ideas, almost any age is acceptable. For current events, especially economic and political information, articles need to be as recent as possible. A quotation about the stock market a month ago isn't relevant today.

Credibility is also simple to understand. Articles must come from a published source. (Private conversations are not published.) Books, government documents, journals, newspapers, and reputable websites can be credible sources, but some are more credible than others. A few newspapers and magazines have fact-checking departments. Academic sources, such as journals and books, send every article out for peer review, so that other experts can find any mistakes before publication. Please use your common sense when evaluating a source's credibility. Is it better to quote a medical doctor or the *Wall Street Journal* about smoking and lung cancer? Which is the better source for information on U.S. economic statistics?

The final quality of a quotation is what matters the most: validity. Most non-debaters believe that what's important is the truth of an argument, but just as good topics are not clearly true or false, many reasonable arguments are debatable. Therefore, to call an argument **valid** is merely to say it is built with good reasoning. No one has a crystal ball into the future or a perfect system for answering moral dilemmas. Thus, valid arguments must be reasonable and logical even though good reasons might turn out to be incorrect. However, an invalid argument is guaranteed to be a loser. Neither side in a debate has to prove absolute truth. Unlike a courtroom, the standard is much lower than "beyond a reasonable doubt." When a judge decides a debate, he looks at which side presents the most valid arguments, not the Truth.

Specifically, what makes an argument valid or invalid?

According to the philosopher Stephen Toulmin, a valid argument ought to have at least four elements: a claim, data, warrants, and relevance. You should be able to point to each of the four elements in your quotation. If you can't, it might be because its argument is invalid. Some invalid arguments are fallacies, illogical missteps that appear to work but fail on a closer and more careful examination. Let's go through the points one-by-one of what makes an argument valid.

The **claim** is the main point that the author makes, the conclusion that he asks us to believe. For example, he might claim that *50 million people are malnourished in the U.S.* or *smoking causes lung cancer*. The first claim is a factual claim. The second claim is a causal claim. Causal claims can be rephrased as "if, then" statements, for example: *if you smoke, then you will be more likely to get cancer*. Causal claims are obviously a little more complicated to prove than factual claims. The third kind of claim is a value claim: *life is more important than money*.

The three kinds of claim represent fundamentally different kinds of argument. As the philosopher David Hume noticed, there is an enormous difference between stating what is or will be (factual or causal) and arguing for what ought to be (value). If your author makes a factual claim and builds a valid argument to support it, you should not use his argument to make a value claim. It would be illogical and invalid, and you harm your credibility.

One article might make several different kinds of claim, but many times, you can guess the main (or only) kind of claim from the publication type. Most newspaper articles are **descriptive** and merely state factual claims, with a few occasional causal claims. In general, descriptive articles are more common. This kind of article can be unbiased and objective, but it is limited in its application in a debate.

On the other hand, prescriptive articles, such as opinion-editorials, advocate value claims, and often include causal claims, too. To quickly find out whether an article is prescriptive, try searching for words such as "should," "ought," or "must." Prescriptive articles are usually much more useful for debate because you can use the author's arguments to support your own advocacy. However, you must be wary of how the author builds her arguments. Prescriptive articles come in different strengths, from rhetorical, analytical, to synthetic. **Rhetorical** articles are the weakest. Instead of offering any good reasons, the author merely gives a well-worded, slick answer. It's drama without substance, and so it's useful only for an opening or concluding flourish to a speech. **Analytical** articles provide clearly stated reasons, often even listing them point-by-point, which can help you support your arguments. **Synthetic** articles are the strongest. The authors discuss different viewpoints, weigh the reasons to believe each, and deliver a final evaluation. They're comparative and allow you to anticipate and beat your opponent's challenges to your argument. Many academic articles are written in this style and are worth searching out.

It seems like the biggest difference between the styles of descriptive, rhetorical, analytical, and synthetic articles is how they use facts.

Yes. Descriptive articles stick to the facts; at the other extreme, rhetorical articles have no facts; analytical and synthetic articles are somewhere in between. Because these styles tend to make different kinds of claims, they have to use facts differently.

To return to Toulmin's idea, every valid argument requires **data**—information—to support its claims. (A grammatical note: "data" is a plural noun. "These are good data" is correct.) Let's say that the U.S. Census Bureau did surveys and came to the conclusion that about 50 million people are malnourished, or let's say that some medical doctors have noticed smokers often get cancer. These are both examples of good data. Data can also include examples, analogies, or historical patterns. However, definitions of words <u>never</u> count as data:

> Data: By definition, God is perfect in every way.
> Definition: Anything perfect must exist because non-existence
>   is a kind of imperfection.
> Claim: Therefore, God exists.

Philosophers made this argument, called an ontological "proof" of God. As you can see, they also used a definition as data, and the whole argument is invalid because it's not based on any real information. We can discuss how we should define words, but redefining words doesn't change anything about the real world.

In most debates, both sides agree on most of the data and instead debate what it is that the data prove. Your opponents might look at the same data but argue that the data support their claim and disprove your claim. Think of it this way: no data are self-evidently clear in meaning; someone must interpret them. This interpretation is the third part of a valid argument: the **warrant**. Think about a mystery novel. "Aha! Here is $5 in your wallet, which means the butler did it!" The missing step of explanation is the warrant. The warrant shows how the data link to the claim:

DATA →	WARRANT →	CLAIM
information →	*how the information supports the claim* →	*conclusion being advanced*
U.S. Census Bureau research →	The researchers analyzed the census data thoroughly and comprehensively. →	50 million people are malnourished in the U.S.
observations of medical doctors →	The research ruled out other factors, such as socio-economic status. →	Smoking causes cancer.

The expertise of your sources is not warrant enough. For example, *doctors know what causes cancer, so we should believe them because of their expertise* is a fallacious warrant, known as an appeal to authority. Even an expert needs to provide a good warrant for any interpretation of what his or her data actually mean. How was an experiment done? How were the statistics gathered? Were research methods typical or atypical? All these can affect the reliability of data. Once we know the data are reliable, we also have to ask ourselves if the data are logically sufficient to support a claim. What if my claim were that we should have a system of universal health care, and my data were all the times I caught a cold recently? You'd be wise to point out that my data are insufficient to make my claim.

This leads us to the final part of a valid argument: **relevance**. Why are you making the argument in the first place? How does the argument connect to the whole debate? Does an argument prove anything we care about? Imagine saying the words, "... and thus I win the debate," after an argument; if it doesn't make sense, then you should probably not bother making that argument. This is only a <u>test</u>, so don't actually say it 50 times in one round and blame it on me.

There is some trade-off between the relevance and validity of an argument: the strongest and most valid arguments are less frequently relevant for debate—what opponent would challenge you on a well-established fact? It is the shakier but still reasonably valid arguments that are the most relevant for a given topic. This is all a part of the excitement of debate. Why bother with easy-to-prove but useless ideas? Go big or go home! This is why synthetic articles, which look at both sides but make one final claim, are the most useful kind. They give you valid arguments about the most relevant issues.

If I do a good job, then I'm done, right?

One caution: you must always keep updating your research. Research is an ongoing process. Learn from your opponents. Revisit the library if your opponents have new and unique attacks. When you finish a round, write down the sources your opponents quote, and be ready to share yours. This is required: debate is about good scholarship and intellectual integrity. If no one is allowed to verify your quotations, they will suspect you made them up. Once armed with your opponents' sources, you can produce quality research more easily when you return to the library. This is an excellent reason to always save your flows.

For the same reason, don't throw your research away at the end of the topic. Save it! **Back files** can be wonderful resources on later topics. When you research a new topic, sift through your back files first before hitting the library. Right now, you're building up a stock of research. The short-sighted view is to think only of this topic, but the long-sighted view is to think of your research as a resource for your entire debate career, whether that spans one or 50 topics. You are becoming an amateur scholar, so you should keep a record of your scholarship.

Review questions:

1. What is a literature review? Why is it so important?

2. Why should you be cautious using Internet sources?

3. What is rabbit-trailing? the S.S.C.I.?

4. What are the qualities of good evidence?

5. Define "claim," "data," "warrants," and "relevance."

6. Why is synthetic evidence the best? Why is analytical evidence better than rhetorical evidence?

Milestone:

Make a list of the resources—databases, government documents, etc.—that you have access to. Look through a back file from your teammates and analyze its quality. Is most of the research rhetorical, analytical, or synthetic? Your coach should also be giving you arguments to analyze for claims, data, warrants, and relevance. And at this point, you should already be researching your first topic for competition. Happy hunting in the library!

CHAPTER 5

Briefing

You still haven't addressed the problem of using my quotations in a round. I got great articles and know what I want to quote. How do I actually use this to win a debate?

Once you've evaluated the quality of your articles and found them to be good, the next step is to get them round ready as **evidence**. How you do this depends on the rules: if your debate competition allows direct quotations (and most do), then you can turn articles into cards. A single direct quotation of a few paragraphs is a **card**. Debaters used to put these quotations on index cards, thus the name "card." You can photocopy the article or book, cut out the relevant passage with scissors, and tape the card onto a blank piece of paper.

If you have your article in electronic format, however, you can cut and paste into a word processor program. E-carding is much more time efficient than printing a paper copy first and physically cutting it up with scissors. The card is also saved permanently on your computer's hard drive. Even if you lose your paper copy, you can print out another. I recommend Scrivener, available on Windows ($40) and Mac ($45). It allows you to save and sort all your PDFs in one place, read your PDFs, copy directly from the PDFs, and then paste quotations into any number of documents (for different arguments) you can have open at the same time, all without leaving the program. Once you've finished all your documents, you can sort them easily into any order and print to paper or PDF any selection of them you want. Or you can save your work into a Word document or rich text file for further editing. Scrivener was designed for authors to write books. It is stable with very, very large documents.

E-carding is also good because it's easier to share an electronic document with teammates than a paper version. Cards are the building blocks of arguments, so why not share them as a team? If your debate competitions do not allow direct quotations, you can paraphrase an article by rewriting the important ideas in your own words; it accomplishes the same purpose.

Here's an example card:

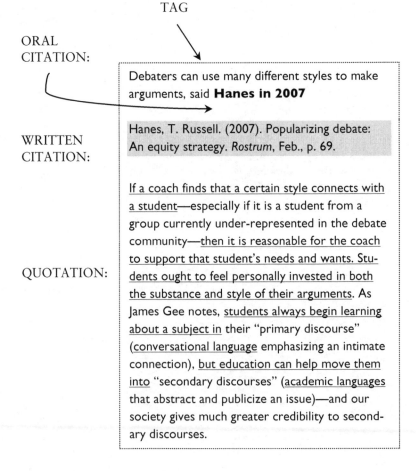

TAG

ORAL CITATION:

Debaters can use many different styles to make arguments, said **Hanes in 2007**

WRITTEN CITATION:

Hanes, T. Russell. (2007). Popularizing debate: An equity strategy. *Rostrum*, Feb., p. 69.

QUOTATION:

If a coach finds that a certain style connects with a student—especially if it is a student from a group currently under-represented in the debate community—then it is reasonable for the coach to support that student's needs and wants. Students ought to feel personally invested in both the substance and style of their arguments. As James Gee notes, students always begin learning about a subject in their "primary discourse" (conversational language emphasizing an intimate connection), but education can help move them into "secondary discourses" (academic languages that abstract and publicize an issue)—and our society gives much greater credibility to secondary discourses.

As you can see, a card has four parts:

1. Tag: A summary of the argument that the card supports. A good tag should be powerful and short. It should be one sentence only, in clear grammar: strong verb, few or no adjectives or adverbs. The tag should accurately capture the author's claim. During a round, you read the tag before reading the quotation to summarize it for the judge's flow.

2. Oral citation: For every quotation, you must say the author's last name and the year of publication, and you can also include the author's qualifications; for example: *Smith, a world famous economist, wrote in 1776.* During a round, you read the oral citation before reading the quotation but after reading the tag to let everyone know that what follows is in fact a quotation and not your original idea. If there are multiple authors, read aloud only the first-listed author. Dictionaries, newspapers, and websites often don't list an author, so you cite the source instead; for example: *Webster's 2011 edition, the New York Times reported in 2015,* or *whitehouse.gov, downloaded in 2014.*

3. Written citation: For every quotation you read, you need to have all the specific publication information for reference, so that a person can track down the quotation. Fortunately, you don't need to read it during a round! The information must be complete, or the card might be thrown out of the round by the judge. The written citation should include all the authors' full names, the month and day of publication if applicable, page number or the name of the database that you downloaded the article from, the source's name or URL (web address), and any other information needed to find the article. Check out the written citation style required for your debate competition: it is usually Modern Language Association (M.L.A.) or American Psychological Association (A.P.A.) style.

4. Quotation: In carding your article, you select only excerpts from the article that make arguments. Most articles give the reader a lot of background before making any real arguments. For example, historical information may be interesting but is

utterly useless for debate. Don't cut cards you won't ever use in a round.

Can I cut a card down to make it shorter?

Never alter or adulterate the quotation. From beginning to end, it should appear exactly as it does in the article: no ellipses, no deletions, and no additions. If you remove sentences from the middle of a card, people will be suspicious that you doctored its meaning. If there are a few words or whole sentences you want to skip over (perhaps because they're repetitive or a tangent), that's fine—just underline or highlight only the parts you want to read aloud. Of course, it's important when underlining that you're merely shortening the quotation, not changing its meaning.

A card might be a few sentences or several paragraphs. You can decide where to begin and end the quotation. I recommend never going shorter than about a paragraph (no headlines, please): arguments require context to make sense. Each excerpt must be complete. If a paragraph doesn't make sense without the one before it, then don't separate them into two cards; leave them together as one card. What matters is quality, not quantity. At the other extreme, a card should fit on a piece of paper; a card should be shorter than the whole article! A good article may have one or a dozen quotable passages—so it might give you one or a dozen good cards. Don't fake it for a few bad cards.

Finally, remember that cards must be quotations that can be spoken aloud. Advertisements, graphs, photos, and tables are unacceptable because they are visual, not verbal, and therefore can't be quoted.

I have good evidence, but I always forget to use my cards during my practice rounds. How can I make my evidence more helpful to me?

To be useful during a round, you need to turn your evidence into briefs. A **brief** is a short set of arguments on one issue that you write as you research. Briefs save you valuable preparation time because you've pre-thought how to explain the issue to the judge. For example, a first affirmative constructive is a long brief that you write before the debate. You think about your advocacy, write down your arguments, and then practice to make sure you can read it within the time limits. On the other hand, an opening negative constructive is pulled together from multiple briefs, a new one for each line of attack. You pre-write all possible attacks, but then choose only applicable ones against a given opponent. You can also write briefs for more than opening speeches. You should write briefs whenever you can anticipate needing to explain multiple arguments on one issue. The best debaters are good researchers who constantly write and edit briefs, saving precious in-round preparation time by making the most of their before-tournament time to research, think, and write.

Briefs use cards, but it is important to mix in your own ideas and analysis to develop the arguments. Your own explanations are known as **analytics**; you provide the claim, data, and warrants in your own words, without quoting a card. In general the best briefs mix cards and analytics evenly: card, analytic, card, analytic, and so on. If your brief is nothing but analytics, you might be tempted to speed through it, but this would be impossible for the judge to flow. If your debate competitions don't allow cards, then your briefs are made of nothing but analytics or paraphrased quotations; just make sure to slow down. On the other hand, if your brief is nothing but cards, it will take too long to read. Analytics can be used if you use arguments that are self-evident and need no card or if you lack a card to support every argument. An evenly mixed brief allows you to make many arguments and support several of them with cards, but it is also easy to read and to flow. A sample brief follows:

Debate High	Education topic
Debater: Hanes	Affirmative ev.

Brief: debate is educational

A. Debate teaches critical thinking skills and helps students learn about politics
B. Debate helps students get into colleges, said Prof. Minh A. Luong
<CARD>

C. Debate is about the only way for students to practice public speaking, a vital skill
D. Debaters are committed to good academic practices, said Prof. Gary Alan Fine
<CARD>

How long should a brief be?

It depends on how complex the set of arguments is. To support simple arguments, you only need a short brief that might fit on one piece of paper, or to support more complex arguments, you want a longer brief that might take up multiple pages. A good brief should bring anyone up to speed on your arguments. Imagine that the judge has no familiarity with your research. How can you get your arguments across in a way that makes sense? You can always find some way to present even the most challenging ideas; never pick an argument solely because it's easy to present. Pick good arguments first and think about presentation second. If your brief is built on bad cards, then your opponent could point this out—and you'll be worse off than if you had said nothing at all. You can't write a good brief from bad cards because a brief merely tells the judge what your arguments are about. A good brief reveals the argument in all its strength and clarity, which means the key qualities of a good brief are transparency, coherency, and word economy.

Does a brief have to be organized like an essay?

Poorly organized briefs confuse judges; too many details can bore them. A brief does have to be organized, but it's written for speaking, not reading. In a way, a good brief is more like a newspaper story than like an essay.

A newspaper story contains all the information necessary for it to make sense, but it's organized in a way that the information is easy to understand and recall. Most use a chronological organization, telling the reader the facts in the order they happened: "At 8:54 pm on Friday, two men in ski masks walked into the Lucky Lab pub on Hawthorne. By 9:10 pm..." You can use this organizational pattern for writing your briefs: start with the current situation, before moving onto possible future events. The chronological organization is best for arguments about causes and effects.

You can also organize your briefs by sub-topics. You've probably seen movies with several unrelated plot lines. The movie jumps from one to another, keeping each separate, until the moment at which they all intertwine. This works for writing briefs: separate your arguments, moving from one sub-topic to another. This works best for briefs where there are only three to six distinct arguments. For example, you might write a brief defending universal health care: *1. Universal health care helps poor people who can't afford insurance; 2. universal health care helps the economy because businesses would no longer need to pay for workers' insurance; and 3. the quality of health care would be as good as under a private health care system.* These are three separate sub-topics.

Third, conflicts organize many fiction and non-fiction stories. This pattern is especially useful in debate, because you are an advocate. In your brief, you first present a problem, and then you propose a solution. For the most part, this is the kind of pattern that helps judges most easily follow and understand the arguments you're trying to present. For example, you might write a brief defending clean air laws like this: *1. Currently, industries release too much greenhouse gas, causing global warming; 2. clean air laws are being amended to include greenhouse gases as air pollution, thus stopping global warming.* There are other ways to organize briefs, but these are the most common.

How complete do briefs need to be? Am I aiming for perfection?

Don't think that you need to answer every possible objection to your argument in your frontline brief. A frontline proposes and initially explains an argument in an opening speech. It's better to wait to see what your opponent chooses to attack before responding. The only exception is if your opponents always make the same attack, you might want to weave a pre-emption to their attack into your initial story. Generally, however, you further develop and strengthen your argument in later speeches with extension briefs. Defending your argument against your opponents' challenges is known as blocking, and any briefs written as such defenses are known as **blocks.**

A block is a collection of responses to fend off your opponent's attack. You write blocks while you're researching because your research allows you to anticipate what attacks your opponent is likely to make. Each block is written for one specific attack. Whenever you hear a new attack, immediately write a new block to use at that competition, and then revise it after you get to do more research. Always continue to rewrite your blocks to be prepared for anything your opponents might throw at you.

However, don't get too carried away with preparing blocks. Why bother writing a fifty-card block? You'd never have time to finish reading it during a debate. This is why you should practice reading each block. How long does it take you to read it? Time yourself, and then write that time in a corner of the paper. When you are pulling blocks together, you can use these notations to tell how many of them you can read in the time limit. Blocks and briefs that are quicker are actually more useful; they have greater word economy. Half-a-dozen arguments are plenty if they are actually good arguments. Quality is more important than quantity.

For the same reason, your best response should always be first on the block; it might be all you have time to read. Finally, good debaters make sure that their blocks do not merely repeat the original argument which is under attack and that the blocks actually continue to develop the argument. Merely restating the original argument is a mistake known as scripting. How you develop the argument may or may not turn out to be a good response to the attack, but repeating the same argument over again is non-responsive. Using these techniques, you can write strong blocks and briefs as you research that save you valuable time during a round. Good briefing and blocking are the keys to solid debating.

What do I do with my briefs and blocks once I write them?

Of course, all these briefs and blocks have to be organized to be useful. Let's say your team has been productive, and you have 100 pages of them. Why do all that research if you can't find it when you need it during a round? If you've only got ten or twenty briefs, you might be tempted to put your evidence in a binder, but it takes too much time to click the binder open, pull out the brief you want, click the binder closed, flip to the next one, click open... You need an organization system that is simple and flexible.

I recommend using letter-sized accordion files, either the 1-21 (alphabetical) or 1-31 (daily) files. They're simple and flexible to use. I put briefs that cover similar issues in the same pocket, using colored paper to make sub-dividers. On the outside of each accordion, tape on an index that lists every brief in each pocket. When you start out, you may have only two accordion files: one for affirmative briefs, one for negative. As you research more, you can easily add new accordions to hold your expanding collection. I also recommend keeping all your flows in a special accordion. Just take all your flows from a round, fold them in half together, and on the outside paper, record your opponents' names and school.

There is another option: electronic filing, also known as paperless debate. The idea is to store all your evidence on the computer and to read all of your briefs and blocks directly from the computer screen. There are several benefits and challenges to electronic filing. One benefit is weight: papers and accordions are heavy, especially if you want to carry around extensive back files with you. On my laptop today, I have every piece of evidence I have researched since sixteen years ago, when I first decided to save everything electronically, and I still have plenty of free hard drive space. A second benefit is that if you can continually edit and improve your blocks during a tournament. On a paper copy, you can only make minor edits before it gets too cluttered.

There are some challenges to going paperless. Some are easy to troubleshoot. Computers do crash, so you need to have your files backed up on an external storage medium (a flash drive or DVD, for example) and access to a backup computer. Rooms don't always have convenient power outlets, so you always need to bring a power strip. Some competitions don't allow the use of computers during a debate, so you should check the rules first.

Other challenges are more difficult to overcome. One challenge is how hard it can be to manage during a debate. If you have ten e-blocks to read, shuffling quickly between them during your speech is difficult. The computer screen can feel more cluttered and confusing than a stack of paper blocks in your hand. There are programs, such as Verbatim, DebateOS, and DebateSynergy, that make it easier to keep track of multiple blocks. Verbatim is based on a Word template. DebateOS is based on a LibreOffice (free) template. DebateSynergy is based on a Word template and a web app. If you bought Scrivener to write blocks from your research, you can also use it in rounds as your electronic filing system.

Furthermore, you must plan for a way to show the blocks you read to your opponents during a debate. You can copy the files on to a flash drive—if your opponents also have computers. Otherwise, you may find yourself loaning them your computer for several minutes while they read your blocks.

The other challenge I see is about preparation. You can write useful notes, ideas, and questions in the margins of a paper block. Keeping everything on paper forces you to be very organized, too.

Marking up an electronic document with text boxes, comments and reviewing, or annotation tools is possible but challenging. Keeping all the different electronic documents organized on your computer is possible but challenging. Here again, Scrivener comes out as the best program because you can write comments about a block in the side panel without it distracting from your main panel, the block itself. Scrivener also allows you to subdivide research into folders in any way that you want. However you choose to organize your files, annotating your blocks is a step that requires discipline and patience.

My personal recommendation is a hybrid system: print out the most important briefs and blocks that you know you will need to read almost every round. File them in accordions. Bring your computer with all your other, rarely used blocks and back files in whatever system works for you. I believe that most debaters will need to print less than fifty blocks and that, in an average round, a debater will only need to use his computer to read an e-block once or twice. It is the best of both worlds.

With a hybrid system, I doubt that you will have more than a few accordions, and you can carry them and a laptop around in your backpack. However, if you find that you must carry many accordions around, you need to get storage tubs—specifically, the Rubbermaid 14-gallon tubs: they are exactly the width and height of a letter-sized accordion file, totally waterproof and nearly indestructible. Bankers' boxes are a cheaper but far inferior substitute; they fall apart easily and do not protect against water damage. You can carry your tub or use a luggage cart if you have several.

Will I ever have to speak off-the-cuff, without briefs?

Yes! You try to write all your blocks and briefs before a debate, but there are always arguments that are impossible to predict. Debate is so much more exciting for those moments of extemporaneous speaking. Whenever you speak without briefs, make sure that you clearly deliver each refutation. The best way to do this is through consistent use of **four-step refutation**:

1. <u>Opponent claim</u>: "They say..." First, give the number of your opponent's argument that you are about to refute, and then give the argument's name. Don't repeat his argument for him;

its name should be condensed to two or three words, such as, "her economy argument," or "his U.N. budget idea."

2. <u>My refutation</u>: "I say..." Now, you state the basic idea of your refutation in a sentence.

3. <u>My warrant</u>: "...because..." Third, explain why the judge ought to believe your refutation more than your opponent's argument.

4. <u>Relevance</u>: "...so I win." Finally, explain why it is your refutation matters. How does it tie to the whole debate?

Four-step refutation is crucial to line-by-line debating. Going through all these steps makes it clear and easy to follow your arguments point-by-point. If your opponent made a decent argument, you'll want to repeat steps 2 and 3 several times with different refutations and a warrant for each. The gold standard is six pointing—providing six separate refutations to one opponent argument—but that's only necessary against excellent arguments.

Is there anything else?

One recommendation: immediately after each debate, completely put away all your evidence. Slipshod refiling is a surefire recipe for disorganization in the next round.

To reiterate, there are five stages to the whole research process:

1. Literature review
2. Targeted research
3. Carding
4. Briefing
5. Filing

Good debaters work carefully through all five stages. Outstanding debaters continually repeat the cycle. Every time they hear new arguments or opponents using different sources, they repeat stages 2 through 5. This is a lesson you should take to heart: research is a continual process. Read, write, rewrite, and repeat!

Review questions:

1.   Define "evidence" and "card."

2.   Define "tag," "oral citation," and "written citation."

3.   What are the purposes of blocks and briefs? How do you write good ones?

4.   What are the benefits and downsides of e-carding and e-briefing? The product may be printed out or not—I am only asking about the writing process.

5.   What are the benefits and downsides of paperless debating?

6.   What are the four steps of refutation?

Milestone:

By now, you should be hard at work making briefs and blocks for your current debate topic! Be sure you are following the correct method for your team (electronic or on paper) and the correct written citation style for your competitions. If you're doing high school cross-examination debate—also known as policy debate—you should see the National Debate Coaches Association's Open Evidence Project: http://www.debatecoaches.org/resources/open-evidence-project. They post dozens of files on the current topic, with cards, blocks, and briefs. It is an amazing, free resource.

Affirmative

It is almost necessary in all controversies and disputations to imitate the wisdom of the Mathematicians, setting down in the very beginning the definitions of our words and terms.... for want of this... we are sure to end there where we ought to have begun...

~ Francis Bacon, *Advancement of Learning*, 1605

How do I defend the topic?

The Affirmative plays the defensive role in a debate, defending the topic. Beginning debaters tend to dive right into a topic and say, "Yes, the topic is always true," before figuring out what examples they want to use to defend it. Consider the topic, *Resolved: The U.N. should reform its finances.* How many different examples are there for this topic? The U.N. could ask member nations to contribute more money, change how it spends its money, or make new accounting procedures. Maybe it needs to create a new U.N. bank or currency. There are dozens of ways. This is on purpose: topics get used every round for a long period of time—sometimes even a whole year. Writers draft topics that relate to multiple examples to avoid repetitive debates. Because there isn't time to debate every example of the topic, the Affirmative picks one example as its case. The Affirmative then writes out its entire first speech based on this case. Think of it like a test case: we can't debate the whole topic in one round, so we debate one example of the topic per round instead. Every round at a competition may be about a different case.

A case on the U.N. topic could either increase or decrease U.N. spending. Obviously, the Affirmative could not defend that the U.N. should <u>both</u> increase and decrease its spending. Defending the whole topic would lead to self-contradiction. This is very common on many topics, which is one reason why we debate cases instead. Therefore, the debate is not about the whole topic. The debate is only about the case the Affirmative chooses:

> If the Affirmative wins its case, then it wins the debate.

When a judge votes Affirmative, he isn't saying, "The topic is true." He is saying, "The affirmative case is on balance good." On the other hand, if the Negative casts doubt on the affirmative case, then it wins the debate. When a judge votes Negative, she isn't saying, "The topic is false." She is saying, "The affirmative case is on balance bad." That the focus of the debate is the affirmative case, and that the rest of the topic is irrelevant, is the theory of **parametrics** (pronounced PAIR-a-meh-TRICKS). The Affirmative is not required to defend the whole topic.

Because the Affirmative gets to pick its example, the Negative only needs to show that this case fails. Once the Affirmative reads its case, the rest of the topic is irrelevant. Let's say that the topic is very narrow, with only two possible cases. (By the way, most topics have more than two possible cases.) The Negative should have arguments ready for both but will use only those that are relevant in a given round. The Affirmative's first speech is pre-written; the Negative should be prepared for multiple contingencies.

Doesn't choosing its case give the Affirmative quite an unfair advantage?

I could see why you might believe this. The Affirmative gets to choose whatever case it wants to present, gets to focus its research before a competition, and can and should walk into a debate round with a pre-written case. The Negative must attack whatever case the Affirmative presents in each round. It can seem unfair. However, the Negative only needs show that the arguments in favor of the case are weak, so it is merely taking arguments apart. It doesn't have to build anything. The Affirmative plays the defensive role in debate, and defense is harder, so parametrics just evens the field.

There is a second reason why the Affirmative is kept in check: the Negative does not have to accept the affirmative interpretation of the topic. The Affirmative could try to catch the Negative off-guard by arguing for some outrageous interpretation. What if the

Affirmative interprets "reform" to mean "leave unaltered"? Obviously, this goes too far, but it has been tried before. Negatives can argue and win if they can prove that the affirmative interpretation is unreasonable, the case does not logically support the topic, or other issues are more relevant to the topic. In other words, the Affirmative gets to make the first interpretation of the topic—but it had better be prepared to defend that interpretation.

The Affirmative has two separate, important **burdens**. First, the case must be argued well and shown to be good. This is known as the substantive debate. Second, the affirmative interpretation of the topic and how the case supports the topic have to be reasonable. This is called the procedural debate. The Negative only needs to win one of them to win the debate because:

> The Affirmative must win BOTH
> the substantive AND the procedural debate to win.

The two burdens are: the case is good, and the case is fair. When cases are argued weakly but fairly, they are known as meatballs (safe but uninspired). When cases are argued well but unfairly, they are known as squirrels (crazy and unpredictable). The best cases are both good and fair.

What makes a case good and fair?

The next chapter explains how to write a fair case. This chapter is about how to write a good case. On the substantive debate, how you write your case will often be dictated by which weaknesses you are ready to defend and which strengths you want on your side. The most important thing is the tricks that you have up your sleeve. As the Affirmative, you have the luxury of time to design your defensive tricks. Use that time wisely. A strong affirmative case is like a puzzle that Negatives never figure out in time.

In **policy debate**, all the topics ask whether a government or some other organization should enact some policy, and the topics are phrased to be evocative of a law or resolution that might come from a legislature. The specific topics depend on the competitions you attend, but policy topics generally look like this:

> Resolved: The United States federal government should cre-
> ate a national health care system.

It is also possible that policy topics could have generic actors:

> Resolved: High schools should increase academic freedom.

With either type, the Affirmative defends the topic with only one specific policy as its case. For example, an Affirmative might say that high schools should give student papers free rein, thus increasing academic freedom.

The main part of a case is to show the advantageousness of the Affirmative's policy over other courses of action. This is the bulk of an affirmative case. The Affirmative first proves its policy has **inherency**. By default, the assumption is that the Negative will defend the **status quo**, the current policy that exists now. The Affirmative cannot argue for a policy that is going to happen in the status quo. If the policy is the status quo, the Affirmative loses because the status quo is supposed to be for the Negative. Of course, it's nearly impossible to lose the inherency issue if you chose your policy wisely. About the only time inherency is a voting issue is when an Affirmative fails to stay on top of the news and advocates a policy that Congress passed overnight.

Next, the Affirmative must demonstrate that its policy produces good outcomes. In a sense, inherency identifies a long-term, structural problem, while the **advantages** show the practical effects of working on these problems. Some advantages are quantifiable. Maybe 50 million people in the U.S. are currently malnourished. Advantages can be unquantifiable, such as unethical corporate behavior or the loss of freedom. But why do we care about starvation or freedom? The **harm** is the argument about why we ought to care. Advantages are the better outcomes from doing the policy; harms are the problems with doing nothing. Finally, the Affirmative must prove that its policy would actually cause the advantages to happen. **Solvency** arguments are those that prove that the advantages would result from the policy.

How do I argue the harms?

Most arguments about harms are based on one of two philosophical frameworks: consequentialism or deontology.

Consequentialism

Consequentialism argues policymakers must look to consequences to determine what we must do. We should do whatever
produces the outcomes we want. It is an exaggeration to say that
consequentialists believe that the ends (goal) justify the means (action), but not much of one. One famous consequentialist philosopher was John Stuart Mill, who argued for **utilitarianism**. We
should enact policies that produce the greatest happiness for the
greatest number of people, like so:

$$(\# \text{ of people}) \times (\text{degree of happiness})$$

$$vs.$$

$$(\# \text{ of people}) \times (\text{degree of unhappiness})$$

If the quantity on top is bigger, then we should do that policy. If
the quantity on the bottom is bigger, then we shouldn't do that
policy.

Another consequentialist idea is the belief that we can weigh
one goal against another. For example, consequentialists might
argue that preserving a little freedom may not be worth the loss of
many lives. On the other hand, a lot of freedom may be worth
more than the preservation of a few lives. We make judgments like
this in our daily lives: would we rather spend money on charity or
on ourselves? In philosophy, this idea of balancing multiple goals
is known as **pragmatism**. To be a bit more precise, pragmatic philosophers would reject systems of moral evaluation, such as utilitarianism, as fallacious. They would prefer a dialogue where each
person can come in with his or her own preferences but also learns
from others.

Cases that claim to be value-neutral usually have a pragmatic
approach. The case may appear objective like a newspaper article.
That is <u>never</u> true. Whereas a newspaper writer may truly not care
about whether a particular law or policy passes, a debater of
course wants his policy to "pass"; he is using a pragmatic justifi-
cation.

Deontology

Deontology is the idea that policymakers cannot pursue noble
goals through terrible means. For example, lifesaving medicines

should not be tested on unwilling or uninformed human subjects. In fact, a deontologist might argue that a good intention is always good no matter how bad the result turns out to be.

The most famous deontologist is Immanuel Kant. He argued for the principle of the categorical imperative, which is a rule that is not dependent on possible outcomes; it is categorical or unconditional. He stated that only a rule that we would wish to use universally—applied to everyone in every circumstance—is moral. Other deontologists take a less drastic stance, but what is common is the focus on the act itself or the intentions behind the action rather than the outcomes. Deontologists tend to think about absolute rights and imperative duties.

How should I organize my case when I'm on the Affirmative?

A case is composed of several briefs, called **contentions.** Typically, the Affirmative divides its arguments into contentions by **stock issues.** Stock issues are the six basic components that you will use to compare your case to the status quo. We already know four: inherency, advantages, harms, and solvency. There are two new ones we'll cover in the next chapter: plan and topicality. Here's an easy mnemonic to remember the six stock issues: HIPSTA. However, the distinctions between the stock issues are not hard and fast, and they sometimes blend together. Organizing by stock issues is an easy way to write a clear, solid case, one that gets the story across simply, but it is not the only way. If you think another organizational pattern is best for your particular case, then try it out.

Let's look at a sample stock issue case from the health care topic. This case starts out its advocacy for a national health care system by addressing the problems in the status quo:

(a) The U.S. Congress will not create a national health care
     system anytime soon. [inherency]

This is clear statement about the status quo. Resist the temptation to spend a lot of time on this part of your case. You should spend no more than one minute of your case developing this argument. The usual next step is for the Affirmative to present its policy. Let's say that the policy is to create a U.S. system modeled on the

Canadian health care system. Now we can move to the next contention: the advantages.

On our health care case, here are two possible advantages that an Affirmative can argue:

(b) Lack of health care causes ten thousand unnecessary deaths per year. [advantage 1]

(c) Furthermore, lack of national health care shifts costs to businesses. [advantage 2]

(d) Paying health insurance costs makes U.S. businesses very vulnerable in the global economy. [advantage 2]

(e) Next year, a global economic downturn will ruin many vulnerable U.S. businesses. [advantage 2]

(f) This will cause an economic depression and massive layoffs in the U.S. [advantage 2]

Advantage 1 is only one card long. The harm is implicit but pretty clear. It is probably going to be argued from a deontological perspective: allowing people to die from preventable causes is immoral. Advantage 2 is four cards. Its harm will probably be argued from a consequentialist perspective.

Finally, an affirmative case will present its solvency. There are usually several arguments addressing various aspects of solvency:

(g) A national health care system would save U.S. businesses from the global downturn.

(h) A Canadian-style system would not be very expensive.

(i) The Department of Health and Human Services (D.H.H.S.) could administer the system successfully.

(j) A Canadian-style system would cover everyone and prevent unnecessary deaths.

These are solid arguments for solvency. Of course, you want to back up each argument with a good card. You want to spend a lot of time making advantage and solvency arguments. For every case, these are its biggest weaknesses. Why are they so vulnerable? Because the policy is a new and untested idea. It's easy to establish facts, like inherency, but it's much harder to prove that a particular policy will have the consequences you intend it to have. Please consider spending half or more of your case building your advantages and solvency.

Please note this case includes 10 arguments. This is a reasonable number. If there are more than 20 arguments, you probably won't be making each one well because each separate argument should be backed up by at least one card. The gold standard for the Affirmative is a **prima facie** case, where the judge knows, at first look and without effort, that the case affirms the topic.

Review questions:

1. Define "case" and "parametrics."

2. Why does parametrics help to create a level playing field in policy debate?

3. What are the two burdens of the affirmative case?

4. Define all six stock issues of a good, prima facie case. Outline a possible case with all six stock issues.

5. Compare and contrast "consequentialism" and "deontology." Give an example of a policy a consequentialist would support but a deontologist would oppose and vice versa.

6. Compare and contrast utilitarianism and pragmatism.

Milestone:

Analyze two or more entire cases. For each one, identify the stock issues and how they are addressed. What are their organizing structures? Are the cases very different in organization or more similar?

Why do policy topics all start with the word "Resolved: ..."?

Because these **resolutions** are meant to ask whether we should do some kind of action; they are not true or false statements but questions about obligation. Remember that there's a big difference between asking what <u>is</u> the situation and asking what <u>ought to be</u> the situation. The Affirmative attempts to prove that we should enact the resolution by advocating an example case. In its case, the Affirmative must advocate a clear, fair policy proposal, known as a **plan**. The Affirmative needs to prove that the plan is better than other policies. These are the two burdens of the Affirmative: advocate a fair plan, and show that it is the better option.

That means all I have to do is pick a good plan, and I'm on my way to writing a good affirmative case.

Well, there's one step to take before you can pick a plan. Every topic is complex enough that there are multiple ways to interpret it. Consider the topic, *Decreasing carbon dioxide emissions is the best policy.* (It's not really a policy topic, but it can illustrate my point clearly.) Does "best" mean cheapest, most thorough, most fair, or something else? How the Affirmative interprets this word changes what policy it should pick. The cheapest plan might be windmills, but the most thorough plan might be electric cars because gasoline powered cars are the single greatest source of carbon dioxide.

Many debaters at this point run to the dictionary to define the topic, but that is the wrong response. No dictionary will ever be sufficient on its own. Why? A dictionary gives you <u>possible</u> meanings for each word, but to understand some words such as "best," you need to understand the whole context of the topic. That means that you can use a dictionary, books, articles, or the Internet to start, but your analysis and arguments about the meaning of the whole topic are just as important.

Therefore, the Affirmative first writes an interpretation of the topic before it writes a case. The reason is simple: the Affirmative must be prepared to defend that its case supports the topic, and this preparation should not be an afterthought. Sometimes, the case idea hits you first, but the point is about the proper order of preparation. The most fundamental question is how the Affirmative thinks its plan is an example of the topic.

Why not write clear topics so we know exactly what they mean?

My theory is that a debatable topic must have at least one ambiguous word. For example, try replacing "best" with a more precise term: *Decreasing carbon dioxide emissions is an environmentalist policy* is not debatable. It is clearly true. "Best," on the other hand, makes the topic debatable <u>because</u> it is ambiguous. Ambiguity creates grounds for both sides to have arguments about the topic. The **grounds** of the topic are all the possible arguments, cases, plans, and negative positions about it. This is my theory, and some people would disagree with it. But it seems to me that ambiguous words allow debaters to debate all the trade-offs that are inherent in making decisions. The Negative has two options: either defeat the case directly or open up new issues. If the Negative argues that the debate should be decided on new issues, then the judge will have to weigh both sides' arguments against each other.

Once it interprets the topic, how does the Affirmative write out a fair plan?

Remember from Chapter 1 the difference between argumentation (the specific ideas) and advocacy (one's overall stance). One key element of a fair plan is that its advocacy is clear: vagueness is a reason for the judge to vote against the Affirmative. You can always adapt your arguments, but the core advocacy of the plan should not change. This doesn't mean the other extreme of over-specifying is necessary. All that the Affirmative needs to do is present a **text** that explicitly defines its advocacy in the first affirmative speech, taking 30 seconds to one minute to read. The text is the affirmative plan; everything else in the case is support, arguments to show that the plan is both fair and good.

Let's look at the health care topic, *Resolved: The United States federal government should create a national health care system*, to see how to write a plan text. Here's a possible plan text:

> In defense of this topic, we offer the following plan: the U.S. federal government should create a national health care system based on the Canadian model. Funding should be through the Medicare budget, with states required to pay the remainder of costs. Enforcement should be through the Department of Health and Human Services.

This is a fair and reasonable plan—just look back to the topic. The plan would use the actor that the topic mandates, the U.S. federal government, and it advocates the action required of creating a national health care system. A fair plan must be **topical**: an example of the topic, based on a reasonable interpretation of the topic.

The best approach to writing a plan is to find an author's proposal or idea and closely model it. This expert is known as your **solvency advocate**. If no expert or author supports an idea, it's probably not a very good one. However, your plan should be simple, straightforward, and written in your own words. Your plan can have multiple **planks**, or elements: for example, specific planks for funding and enforcement.

Now, the Affirmative can tinker with its arguments, providing new ones or dropping old ones, but the plan text is its core advocacy:

> The plan text is the core affirmative advocacy.

It is unacceptable for the Affirmative to shift its advocacy during the debate. Cutting planks out is known as **severance**, while adding new planks is known as **spiking**. All the Affirmative can do is clarify its plan a little—but not too much, otherwise it'll be accused of being vague from the start. In fact, sometimes even adding or subtracting one word from the plan text is too much. The Affirmative must stick to its plan throughout the whole debate without spiking or severing. This is the point of having a text. The Affirmative should be able to point to the text throughout the debate, from the first speech to the final rebuttal, to show that its advocacy has never varied.

If the affirmative case is substantively weak, then the Negative just points out the flaws. What if the affirmative plan is unfair?

The first way that the plan could be unfair is if the Affirmative misuses a simple word in the topic. Most of the words in the topic are nouns or verbs. These definitions are factual questions answered by examining trusted dictionaries and academic research. For example, is the European Court of Justice part of the U.N.? (no) Is the World Health Organization part of the U.N.? (yes) If the Negative can prove these words were misinterpreted, then the plan is not an example that is relevant to the topic. This issue is known as **topicality**. Because the Affirmative gives only one plan, if the Negative proves the plan is irrelevant to the topic, it means a loss for the Affirmative. Both sides must be prepared to debate the topicality of a case, which Chapter 12 details.

One key note: topicality applies only to the plan text. No other arguments in the case have to be topical; they merely need to be tied to a topical plan.

> The plan text, and ONLY the plan text, must be topical.

For example, advantages may be anything that result from the plan. Helping the economy may be an advantage to universal health care. Even though this benefit is not topical itself, this is an acceptable advantage; all that the Affirmative must do is show that its health care plan would solve economic problems.

Can the Negative argue that the plan is impossible?

No. It may surprise you, but for the purpose of a good debate, we pretend that the Affirmative has the power to put its plan into action. Whether the plan can actually be passed is irrelevant to policy debate. In some forms of policy debate, the Affirmative is actually known as the government side, meaning the Affirmative can "enact" its policy. This is an idea known as **fiat**.

Why do debaters pretend the plan happens? Two reasons: First, inherency proves that the affirmative plan will definitely <u>not</u> happen in the real world. The Affirmative would be contradicting itself if it argued its plan could be done. Second, we don't want to discuss the world as it is or will be. We want to debate what it <u>ought to be</u>. The only way to do this is for the debaters and judges to assume hypothetically that the plan will go into effect. Fiat focuses the debate on whether a policy would be good instead of whether it could be done. Imagine that a debate round is actually happening on the floor of Congress, with the plan at a tied vote. In fact, some people like to think of the judge as the swing vote in Congress. When speaking in a debate, use the conditional mode— "The plan would..."—but in thinking, assume that the plan will happen.

The Negative and the judge agree to pretend that the Affirmative is the government and that the affirmative plan becomes law?

Exactly right. However, this metaphor extends only so far:

> In defense of this topic, we offer the following plan: the U.S. federal government should create a national health care system, with the Republicans proposing the plan in the subcommittee, with the measure coming to a floor vote that should be tied with the Vice-President voting as a tiebreaker.

The Affirmative does not get the power to control each member of the government like a robot; the Affirmative can "pass" its plan but does not get to be omnipotent. Do I need to go on? It is called fiat abuse, and it is the second way that the affirmative plan can be unfair.

Why is it unfair?

This tactic focuses on "How is the plan passed?" instead of "Is the plan good?"—but the whole point of fiat was to skip over the first kind of question to focus instead on the second. In other words, this over-use of fiat is counter-productive to the purpose of fiat. To debate the effects of the plan, we make an assumption (plan passes) that also has smaller assumptions tied to it (for example, it passes next week). However, we want to keep our assumptions as limited as possible. In other words, your plan should use **normal means** wherever possible.

> The plan should happen as any similar bill, treaty, or policy would happen.

Getting into too much detail can be a way of abusing fiat power.

There are other ways to over-use fiat power that are also unfair and abusive:

> In defense of this topic, we offer the following plan: the U.S. federal government should create a national health care system based on the Canadian model with funding through cutting the military budget by 50%.

Whether cutting military funding is a good or bad idea, there is no connection to the topic of health care. The topic limits fiat power. In the good example plan I gave, the plan used Medicare to provide funding, which is one way that the government might raise money for health care, but cutting the military isn't. The Affirmative can properly claim fiat only for what is necessary and normal means for the creation of a health care system. By cutting the military budget, the Affirmative has really provided a second plan, one that is not topical to boot. We call this second plank of the plan **extra-topical** (outside the topic's scope), and it is unfair.

Is there any way that the Affirmative can use too little fiat power to enact its plan?

Sort of. Imagine that this example is the Affirmative's whole plan:

> In defense of this topic, we offer the following plan: the U.S. government should require everyone to buy health insurance.

The Affirmative might argue that nearly everyone will comply and buy insurance, and that this is sort of a national health care system. This kind of plan is known as **effects topical**: the plan itself is not topical, even though the Affirmative tries to argue unfairly that its advantages can somehow make it topical. Remember: it is the plan text—not the advantages or anything else—that must be topical. The plan must be **on-face topical**. In this example, the judge can't answer whether everyone will have health care without looking at the solvency. That is the problem. The Affirmative has tried, unfairly, to **mix the burdens** of the case by blurring the lines between solvency and topicality. The affirmative plan is simply not adequate on its own. It is under-using its powers of fiat because it is not doing the action the topic requires.

How does the Negative respond when the Affirmative abuses its fiat power?

By attacking topicality if the plan is extra-topical or effects topical. What word in the topic gives the Affirmative power to fiat a military budget cut? None. How does the Affirmative create a national health care system? It doesn't. If the Negative can win topicality, then the plan is thrown out, and because the Affirmative can't offer a new one, the Negative wins. Sometimes, the Affirmative abuses fiat by ignoring normal means, treating Congress like a collection of robots or using fiat in some other absurd way. In these situations, the Negative should make a procedural argument about fiat abuse. Chapter 12 details how to make both topicality and procedural arguments.

Review questions:

1. Explain how a completely unambiguous topic might not create sufficient grounds for one side or the other to have a fair debate. Give several examples.

2. Define "plan," "text," "planks," and "extra-topical."

3. Why is having a solvency advocate (or near-advocate) a good idea?

4. Give an example each of severing and spiking a plan. Explain why these practices are not fair.

5. Explain why only the plan text, and not the advantages, must be topical. Explain why effects topicality is not fair.

6. How does fiat change and improve the debates we can have? What is normal means, and why is it a necessary limit on fiat?

Milestone:

Now it is your turn. Write your own plan. Make the text straight-forward, fair, and strategic. Outline the entire case around it. Take the time to make your affirmative case something you can take to your first competition!

Negative

Neither grammatical subtleties nor ingenuity in weaving words or arguments help me... They are all right for the classroom... where we are free to doze off and find ourselves a quarter of an hour later still with time to pick up the thread of the argument. I want arguments that drive home their first attack right into the strongest point of doubt.

~ Michel de Montaigne, *Essays*, 1580

I understand that the Affirmative gets to choose the case for a round, so what does the Negative get to do? Why isn't the Negative really at a disadvantage?

The Affirmative gets to choose the plan by its lonesome, and all the Negative can do is speculate about what the Affirmative might argue. However, remember that the Negative only needs to attack the Affirmative case, not the whole topic. The Negative only has to show that the Affirmative hasn't met its burden of proof. The Negative gets to play the destructive role, which means the Negative can have a laser-like focus on just a few arguments against each case. In debate, as in everything else, defense (Affirmative) is harder; the Negative always has options on how it attacks.

I've heard debaters talk about off-case and on-case arguments. Is there a difference?

The main distinction is whether the negative argument is made to take apart the affirmative case (on-case attack) or to present a new objection that is not refuting a case claim (an off-case position or issue). This chapter describes the on-case attack, also known as "case neg." While you can attack the weaknesses in the affirmative case, you should also attack weaknesses arising from what the case omits to talk about. For example, maybe the case doesn't mention its cost, but you know that the cost will be quite expensive. The Negative should try to shift the debate to its off-case positions while simultaneously making on-case attacks to prevent the Affirmative from bringing the debate back to the case. Therefore, debaters usually refer to on-case attacks as defensive and off-case attacks as offensive, but this isn't a hard rule. Off-case negative arguments fall into four general types:

1. <u>Counterplans</u> (Ch. 9): arguments that while the plan might be good, there's something better. Specifically, the Negative can present an alternative to the plan, a counterplan.

2. <u>Critiques</u> (Ch. 10): arguments that while the case might be true, it overstates its own moral importance.

3. <u>Disadvantages</u> (Ch. 11): arguments about bad consequences of the plan. On balance, are the disadvantages worse than the advantages are good?

4. <u>Topicality</u> (Ch. 12) and other attacks on the fairness of the affirmative advocacy: Is the plan fair? ("No" is fiat abuse.) Is the plan a relevant example to the topic? ("No" is a topicality attack.)

You can argue any combination that you want. For example, perhaps you could run a topicality attack, a disadvantage, and a good counterplan. This gives you three viable options for the final rebuttal. You can get rid of the ones that aren't working as the debate progresses ("Ok, never mind, plan is topical, but the Affirmative still hasn't shown that..."). Furthermore, it is usually a good strategy to have a mix. Three topicality attacks is not the strongest strategy. But you can do it if you want and if the case is weak on topicality.

The Negative can present as many **positions**, or major issues that are off-case, as it wants. Of course, there is always the time limit. How many positions are good for the Negative? Why waste your precious time in early speeches presenting a terrible position that you know has no hope of ever winning? Instead, you should give yourself a few viable options. But this is all part of the flexibility and choice that the Negative has. There is a lot more creativity and spontaneity in negating—and there is the element of surprise.

You can also consider setting up traps, using one position as a decoy for another. For example, the Negative may argue a weak position, hoping for a certain response that would get the Affirmative into a lot of trouble. This may mean that the strongest Negative arguments don't come out until the second negative speech, or ever, if the Affirmative is too smart or just too dumb lucky to avoid walking into the trap. This means that the original negative position may stand throughout the entire debate, so even though it might be a weak position, it shouldn't actually hurt the Negative. Crafting traps is one of the greatest joys in debate. In summary, although the Affirmative chooses the plan it wishes to defend, it is often the Negative that gets to decide what is actually debated.

How do I attack the affirmative case directly?

There are two basic ways to refute arguments in a debate: (1) show that your opponent's argument is invalid or (2) show that your opponent contradicts himself. In other words, you can show that your opponent's argument fails to demonstrate that the claim is probably true, or you can show that your opponent makes an argument that is opposed in its claim or relevance to another argument he has already made in the round. Contradict literally means "to speak against oneself."

There are three basic techniques for showing that an argument is invalid. The first technique is quite blunt: directly attack the data upon which your opponent's claim rests. An example would be arguing that the data for global warming are faulty. This is the weakest kind of attack because it takes a lot of speech time, so this technique is best used in cross-examination. This is how you do it: read aloud the weak parts of your opponent's evidence during cross-examination and point out all the flaws in the data. See what her response is. If anything is rebutted poorly, bring it up in your next speech.

The second technique to invalidate your opponent's argument is to **subsume** it: rather than disagree with the data behind her argument, you provide an alternate interpretation of the data. In other words, concede the data but refute the warrants. For example, you might say, "Yes, it is historically true that we have never used our nuclear arsenal; however, that merely proves my point that stockpiling these weapons has been an effective deterrent because..." Another technique is for you to hypothetically assume that your opponent's argument is true and follow it to its logical conclusion to show this conclusion is absurd. This shows that the argument is flawed: "Let's pretend for a minute I were to concede your argument X. Well, if X were true, then it would mean Y has to be true, too. Because Y is obviously ludicrous, it shows that X can't be true." This is known as the method of false position— "agreeing" with your opponent's argument for a moment in order to prove it false. This is also known as the *reductio ad absurdum*; taking the idea to its logical end shows how absurd it truly is. These techniques of spinning warrants are an excellent use of your limited speech time.

Third, you can also show that your opponent's reasoning is invalid. Here are a few fallacies (faulty arguments) that frequently appear in debate:

1. Straw manning & false dichotomies: Straw manning is when your opponent puts words in your mouth—because he has lots of answers to these positions he purports you said (and possibly none to better arguments). False dichotomies are similar: *You either support my plan or you endorse killing puppies.* Oh, no! But I love puppies! These are tactics to distract the judge (and you) from what's really important, so keep digging.

2. Backwards cause & effect: Think about the terrible problems of illiteracy and poverty. Are people illiterate because they are poor and education is expensive, or are they poor because they are illiterate and unable to find good work? Both could be true. Your opponent assumes cause and effect runs one direction; you might be able to show that it could plausibly run the other direction.

3. Equivocation, ambiguity, & manipulative language: These word-games show that something deeper is wrong with the case and are a good point of attack. Equivocation is where words are used with multiple meanings, obscuring what is actually going on. Ambiguity is where the meaning is just plain hard to follow. Manipulative language tugs on the heartstrings without presenting solid arguments, for example, by giving a story rather than any data: *Imagine your grandmother starving when she has no more Social Security.* Politicians are noto-

rious for using these techniques in debates. These language tricks cover up serious flaws.

4. Circular reasoning: This is sometimes known as begging the question, where it is assumed what should have been asked. For example, circular reasoning might look like this: *Important people drive nice cars, because nice cars are for important people.* I simply assumed what I should have worked to prove. These kinds of flawed thinking conceal a very weak point in reasoning.

5. False analogies & cherry picking: A false analogy is where your opponent compares the situation to something else, but the comparison does not make sense. Cherry picking is when your opponent picked one example that is not representative of the whole. The fallacy of composition is assuming that what is true of one example is true for a whole group; the fallacy of division is assuming that what is true of the whole group will be true for every part. If they couldn't even find a good example or analogy, perhaps the whole argument is flawed.

These are ideas to get you thinking but are by no means an exhaustive list. There are many other fallacies that you might find in a case.

What about contradictions? What do I do in that situation?

There are two ways your opponent could make this mistake. First, your opponent might very foolishly make two competing claims, such as *This proves the U.N. is under-funded* and *This proves the U.N. has a healthy budget.* This is sometimes known as a **double bind,** and you want to point it out: "Either he wins A or B, but he can't win both." You want to force your opponent's hand: choose for him so that he's stuck with the worse option. This is known as an "even if" argument: "Even if he wins A, he still loses the round, because winning A proves that he loses B." (A small note: please never call contradictions "paradoxes." A paradox occurs when two arguments, even though they seem to be contradictory, must both be true. A paradox is <u>not</u> anything that you happen to find mysterious or an ordinary contradiction.)

Second, your opponent might make a less foolish but still damaging mistake by giving two arguments that, if both true, have opposite relevance. For example, *The U.N. is under-funded* and *The U.N. has limited responsibilities* are not contradictory claims because both could be true, but it is unlikely that one debater wants to make both in the same round! In this situation, you want to make a **strategic concession**. Rather than disagree with the claim, data, or warrants of your opponent, use one of her arguments to take out the other. For example, you might say, "Grant her argument that the U.N. has limited responsibilities, so it doesn't really matter whether it's under-funded or not." In this same vein, you can always simply argue that an argument is irrelevant: "Even if my opponent wins that the U.N. could do a lot more with several billion dollars, I still win the debate because the costs outweigh the benefits..." This is a devastating argument against many affirmative cases: so what?

So both the Affirmative and Negative are held to the same standard about self-contradiction?

One fascinating question in debate right now is whether Negatives can run contradictory arguments. A perfect example is given by a joke about a broken kettle described by Freud: "Firstly, I never borrowed a kettle from [him] at all; secondly, the kettle had a hole in it already when I got it from him; and thirdly, I gave him back the kettle undamaged" (*Jokes and the Unconscious*, 1905). Is this strategy of self-contradiction permissible for the Negative in a debate round?

One side, which believes in **negation theory**, says yes. The idea is that the Negative does not advocate anything; its job is merely to tear the affirmative advocacy apart. The other side believes that the Negative should advocate its positions, and if it has contradictory positions, then it should lose. These debaters argue that it makes affirming impossibly difficult: to answer contradictory negative positions, the Affirmative would have to contradict itself. In other words, it is a trap in the extreme: damned if you do, damned if you don't. In general, negation theory is for the advanced debater, and beginning debaters should run mutually consistent positions on the Negative.

How can I use these ideas to make a complete negative strategy?

All good refutations are basically one of these five techniques. You can attack the data (direct refutation); you can attack the warrants (subsumption) or find fallacies; you can attack the claim (double bind); or you can attack the relevance (strategic concession). Subsumption is a stronger technique than direct refutation, and a strategic concession is far more likely to succeed than a double bind. The better technique of each pair allows you to make a large effect with little effort, rather than get sucked into argumentative quagmires that you have no chance of winning. This is why debate is all about flexible and adaptable argumentation rather than brute force. Good strategizing is a skill that takes experience to develop. I can't tell you, "This is a good strategy," and "That's a bad strategy," because it all depends on the flaws of a particular affirmative case. All I can do is provide you principles to guide you as you try out different strategies.

Principle 1: Be infinitely variable.

Every debate is different. You may be hitting the same opponent, running the same case, even in front of the same judge (sounds like a practice round...), but no matter what, the round unfolds differently each time. The worst strategy is to blindly reuse the strategy of the last round over again. First, small differences hugely change the debate that happens. Is the affirmative case exactly the same? Even a minor case change—for example, one word changed in the plan text—can result in a whole different debate. Second, as a Negative, you don't want to be predictable. Your biggest advantage is surprise, so why would you give it up? If the Affirmative knows what is coming, they can lay traps for you, instead of the other way around.

On the other hand, there isn't enough time to write an entirely new strategy for every single round. You should choose at least a few negative positions that can be used against multiple affirmative cases. These **generic** negative positions may not always apply, but they will apply often enough to save you significant preparation work. You can adapt and modify these positions to fit each case appropriately without starting over from scratch every time. Don't spin your wheels prepping excessively; focus your preparation where it means the most. Attack similar cases using similar strategies but fine-tune the details.

Principle 2: Strategize backward in time.

Novice debates tend toward issues of parenthetical importance. Don't be distracted by the minor details of the case. It is a common mistake for beginning debaters to be sucked into arguments just because they can refute them, rather than because the arguments are important. If there are 50 million malnourished people or if it's only 35 million, it doesn't change the strategic layout of the round. Both are very bad. You don't want to appear to be bickering, so don't waste your time. You need to have a strategy: some attack that will take out the whole case. Every argument you make should support that strategy.

You should always have that strategy in mind from the beginning. It's a backward planning process; you should know the final overview you want to give in your final rebuttal, so work back to the first constructive. However, you must hide your strengths from your opponent. The Affirmative should not know what the actual negative strategy is until it is too late. You need to have double vision: keep an eye on the whole round, while making enough refutations on the line-by-line to win these arguments. Of course, Principle 1 tells you that if it becomes clear that your original strategy isn't working, then you should change immediately to a <u>new</u> strategy. A good test is to ask yourself whether the phrase "and therefore you should vote Negative" makes sense after each argument. If the words would seem like a non sequitur, then you need to rethink your strategy.

Principle 3: Attack weaknesses, not strengths.

This isn't to say that you can ignore the case's strengths, but they should be of secondary concern. The Negative needs to show how the case's strengths are overblown, but it should focus its time on showing major flaws of the case. After all, the Affirmative knows its case very well and is happy to spend its time overstating the case's strengths rather than improvising defenses of its major weaknesses. The best approach is sword-and-shield, combining defensive and offensive arguments together. There's a constant tug-of-war in a round between on-case attacks (affirmative offense, negative defense) and off-case positions (affirmative defense, negative offense). Each side should spend more time on its offense than on defense; the most common mistake in debate is doing the opposite and spending too much time defensively answering arguments that gain you little chance of winning the round.

Finally, you need to be aware that arguments and positions may interact. If you run three disadvantages, there's a strong possibility of overlap. Perhaps the Affirmative is able to make one argument and use it against all three disadvantages, saving precious time. Or worse, the Affirmative may be able to point out that your positions are contradictory. Or the Affirmative may argue that negation theory is unfair and argue for the Negative to lose for bad advocacy. When strategizing, please make sure that all your positions can co-exist.

This all sounds well and good if I anticipate my opponent's case and have planned for it days in advanced. What do I do if I'm hearing a case for the first time as my opponent is saying it in my round? That would freak me out.

Yes, this can be an unnerving situation. Some formats of debate (namely, Parliamentary) force this situation by announcing the topic only 15 minutes before the start of each debate round. Whether it's by the design of your format or by your opponent's cleverness, your response must be the same. Step (1) is to keep your cool. Panicking won't help anything. Don't worry about following every specific detail of the case. Just focus on getting the main gist of it.

Step (2): recognize that all the principles I just listed above still apply. You should have generic arguments already prepared. Do any of them apply to this case? This is why having generic positions is so important. If nothing is coming to mind, flip through your files. Almost certainly, something will grab your attention as an option. Can you shift the debate away from the Affirmative's offense with this position? You probably do in fact have a generic position that applies already in your files. If you thought about the topic thoroughly, you covered the basics. This case might be surprising and different—in some detail or another—but probably not in the essential nature of the plan or the case advantages.

Review questions:

1. Explain the difference between on-case attacks and off-case positions. Why are off-case positions so important?

2. Describe the four types of off-case position. Give an example of each.

3. Compare the strengths and weaknesses of attacking data, subsuming warrants, or showing fallacies in reasoning.

4. Explain double binds and strategic concessions. Give an example of using each one.

5. What are arguments in favor and against negation theory?

6. Explain the three principles of good negative strategy. How can a Negative use generic positions effectively, considering the three principles?

Milestone:

Analyze an affirmative case from top to bottom. For every claim, decide whether you would attack the data, subsume the warrants, show fallacies, argue a double bind, or make a strategic concession. Figure out how to attack the weaknesses of the case and how to waste less time futilely wearing down its strengths.

The Negative wins if it presents a counterplan?

Oh my yes. In fact, these alternatives to the affirmative plan are the most powerful offensive strategy of all because the Negative takes control of what the debate is going to be about. It is no longer about the plan on its own terms but about the plan in comparison to an alternative the Negative chooses.

Counterplans are allowed in some formats of debate but banned in others. However, counterplans are a core part of debate theory, and it is important for every debater, on whatever kind of topic, to understand them. We tackle counterplans first among negative strategies because counterplans are so important.

What does a counterplan look like?

Remember the health care topic, *Resolved: The United States federal government should create a national health care system.* Let's say the affirmative plan is for the federal government to provide insurance through a Canadian-style system. One possible counterplan is for the state governments to provide insurance:

> All 50 state governments, plus the local governments of U.S. territories and commonwealths, should provide comprehensive health care through a system based on the Canadian model.

This looks like a good counterplan. This kind of counterplan is known as an **agent** counterplan, meaning that the counterplan and the plan would do exactly the same thing (Canadian-style system); the only difference is that a different government actor would do the same action (state vs. federal). Depending on the topic, a different nation, a different branch of government, or a different agency could also be suitable for agent counterplans.

The other kind of a counterplan is known as a **process** counterplan. In a process counterplan, the government actor would be exactly the same, but the action or process would be different. For example:

> The U.S. federal government should create a national health care system based on the British model.

This is also a good counterplan. You should have noticed that both counterplans had a text, just as an affirmative plan has a text. You should take care when you write your counterplan text that is clear and fair. Just as with a plan text, counterplan vagueness can become a crucial issue that results in a loss.

Ok, then how do I write a counterplan?

A counterplan should have **net benefits** when it is compared to the plan. Net just means "on balance." In other words, the counterplan should be, on balance, better than the affirmative plan. Usually, the Negative chooses to run a counterplan because the affirmative plan is too strong to take down without providing an alternative. Let's say the affirmative case has one huge advantage. The Negative could devise a counterplan that also results in this advantage—but reaps some additional advantage as well. In a way, the Negative is making some strategic concessions—admitting that part of the case is good—while trying to spin the debate to its advantage. There are two routes to establishing the net benefits of any counterplan:

1. Counterplan also results in the affirmative advantages: This is the defensive part of the counterplan that captures part (or all) of the benefits of the affirmative case. It is even possible for the counterplan to have better solvency than the affirmative plan.

2. Counterplan results in some additional advantages, or it
    avoids disadvantages: This is the offensive part of the coun-
    terplan that sells the net benefits. Perhaps the plan helps the
    homeless but costs so much money that it bankrupts the gov-
    ernment, while the counterplan also helps the homeless (has
    solvency for the affirmative advantage) while costing a frac-
    tion of the amount plan costs (avoiding the disadvantage of
    financial bankruptcy).

Counterplans need to try to do both to establish a net benefit over
the plan. The judge will look at whether the balance of benefits
and risks is better for the plan or for the counterplan.

Because a counterplan is trying to capture most of the affirmative advantages, you want to write your counterplan text in a way
that highlights the key differences, so:

> Word your counterplan text similarly to the affirmative plan text.

If a counterplan does exactly the same action as the plan but with
one minor change, then everyone knows what to focus on. You
want the important difference—such as the federal government's
vs. the state governments' effectiveness—to be as clear as possible.
In other words, make all other things equal except the key difference by copying your opponents' plan text as closely as possible.
This means changing the counterplan text every time, but it is
worth it.

Can the Negative present two counterplans at once?

This is a question of whether the Negative must always advocate
its counterplan, which goes back to the question about negation
theory. If you believe in negative advocacy, the Negative can run
only one counterplan during a round, and if the counterplan is
bad, it loses the debate. On the other hand, some debaters argue
for **conditionality**. Conditionality is the idea that the Negative is
merely testing the Affirmative with the counterplan. If the Affirmative proves that the counterplan is bad, the Negative may still
win by proving that the affirmative plan is bad in some other way,
such as with a disadvantage. Under the conditionality assumption,
the Negative may run as many counterplans as it wishes in the

round—even contradictory ones. Counterplan conditionality is far more controversial and far more difficult to justify than counterplan advocacy and can be challenged by the Affirmative. But, it is possible to make arguments for conditionality, especially if the counterplans are not contradictory.

Affirmative fiat is limited by the resolution, so does that mean the Negative can write any counterplan it wants because it is not limited by the topic?

Good question. Unless there is a check on counterplans, then the Negative could come up with outrageous alternatives, proposing to end world hunger rather than create a health care system—and obviously, ending world hunger would be net beneficial.

What sets the limit is that the counterplan must be a relevant alternative to the plan. For example, consider a debate about dinner. If you say, "Let's have pizza," and I say, "Let's retire in Cyprus," we're not really answering the same question. The Negative attacks the Affirmative and must show that the plan is a bad idea. The desirability of retiring in Cyprus is irrelevant to whether we should have pizza tonight. You would win because you addressed the question and I did not. This is what sets the limit on counterplans.

Providing an alternative, even an awesome one that would end world hunger, prevent all wars, and eradicate all diseases, does not prove that the plan is bad. Even if you say, "Pizza is good," and I say, "Lasagna is better," I would not have proven that pizza is bad. You could always counter with, "Let's have both." Why not? If pizza is good (you say) and lasagna is better (I say), then combining them together would be better than either alone, or at least as good as pizza alone. Having lasagna on the table doesn't detract from the pizza. If I'm going to win our dinner debate, I also need to prove that we can only choose one or the other. I might say, "Two dinners is too expensive," or, "Having both pizza and lasagna is too fattening." Only if we must choose does the fact that lasagna is better come into play. Now I have shown something bad about eating pizza—we lose the opportunity to eat lasagna, which, of course, is better.

This is an idea economists call opportunity cost: we must consider every decision in terms of not only what we gain but also what we lose. In debate, we refer to this as **competitiveness**. By doing the plan, we lose the opportunity of doing the counterplan. If the affirmative plan were to legalize drugs, we could still enact a counterplan to disarm our nuclear arsenal at the same time, so this disarmament counterplan is not competitive and loses. On the other hand, the legalization plan would cost us the opportunity to increase penalties for drug crimes. This is **mutual exclusivity**, when the counterplan and plan can't possibly happen together. Either we increase or decrease penalties for drug crimes but not both—so the *increase penalties* counterplan is competitive. If the Negative cannot show mutual exclusivity, then the Negative must use some alternate strategy to show competitiveness, perhaps arguing that a combination is not good (*fattening dinner*) or not realistic (*expensive dinner*).

So any competitive counterplan is fair?

In general, yes, but some judges and debaters believe that some specific types of competitive counterplans are unfair. For example, many judges believe that every counterplan must be non-topical. Their view is this:

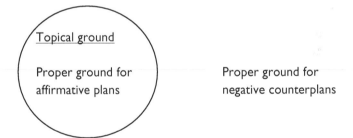

Topical ground

Proper ground for affirmative plans

Proper ground for negative counterplans

According to this theory, everything within the circle is fair game for affirmative plans; everything outside is thus fair game for negative counterplans. This does make some intuitive sense. The argument is that a topical counterplan would be a reason to vote for the topic because a topical negative counterplan could be presented as a regular affirmative plan in another round.

The other school of thought is that counterplans do not need to be non-topical. These judges believe that once the Affirmative picks its plan, everything else, including the parts of the topic the Affirmative did not use, is fair game for the Negative. I side with these judges. The plan text is the focus of the debate. If you decide to present a topical counterplan, then you need to point out that the plan, not the resolution, is the focus of your attack.

Another question is about whether there is a limit to how similar a counterplan can be to the plan. Remember I said the counterplan text should be similar to the plan text except for the key, highlighted difference. Imagine the plan were *The U.N. will spend $50 million fighting AIDS in Liberia, Cote d'Ivoire, and Ghana.* Would a counterplan that says *The U.N. should spend $50 million fighting AIDS in Liberia and Cote d'Ivoire only* be fair? Some judges would say yes, some no. This type of counterplan is known as a **plan-inclusive counterplan** (PIC). It is a question still open to debate.

How does the Affirmative answer a counterplan?

Defensively, the Affirmative can argue that the counterplan is not net beneficial. Procedurally, it could argue that the counterplan is unfair in the ways we discussed before. The Affirmative has a third option, which is offensive. It can argue that the counterplan is not competitive. A non-competitive alternative is an irrelevant alternative. A good alternative is not reason enough to reject the affirmative plan; opportunity cost must be proven to show that the affirmative plan is inadequate. Therefore, the Affirmative wants to show that there is no opportunity cost to its plan. The critical question in every round is, "Compared to what?" With a counterplan, this question becomes, "Must we choose between the plan and the counterplan, or is this a false dichotomy?"

How does the Affirmative do this? By a simple test: can the plan and counterplan be combined? If the Affirmative shows that a combination is possible, then a comparison of the plan to the counterplan is moot, and the judge votes Affirmative by default. Who cares if lasagna is better when we can eat both?

This combination is a **permutation**, which for a counterplan means:

> <u>All</u> of the affirmative plan <u>plus</u>
> <u>part or all</u> of the negative counterplan.

No more, no less. Just as a counterplan has a text, so must a permutation have a text to avoid vagueness.

The Affirmative cannot get rid of any part of its case advocacy in a permutation because this would be admitting that its plan was partly bad. Subtracting elements is known as a **severance** permutation, which is not a fair test of competitiveness. On the other hand, the Affirmative may not add any new elements not in the plan or the counterplan to its permutation. This is known as a **non-intrinsic** permutation. To do so would be for the Affirmative to admit that its original case was inadequate; therefore, a non-intrinsic permutation is not a fair test of competitiveness. Both severance and non-intrinsic permutations are considered unfair and do not provide offense against counterplans.

Does the Affirmative advocate the permutation? In other words, does the affirmative advocacy switch from the plan text to the permutation text? I think the answer is "no," but some judges might disagree with me. The Affirmative is trying to show that the counterplan does not compete; once it does not compete, then the counterplan is irrelevant and so is the permutation. On the other side, is the Negative stuck with its alternative if there is a permutation; in other words, is a good permutation an automatic loss for the Negative? **Dispositionality** is the idea that the Negative can drop its counterplan <u>if and only if</u> the Affirmative shows that a permutation is possible. Under this notion, the permutation moots out the counterplan but not any other negative arguments, which means the Negative could still win. The proponents of this view often argue conditionality is unfair because it is too strong, whereas dispositionality gives the Negative a reasonable burden of advocacy—to continue advocating a counterplan unless it is shown to be irrelevant and moot. Other judges argue that nothing less than full advocacy of the counterplan is acceptable. To summarize affirmative responses to counterplans:

1. <u>No net benefit</u>: Explain how the affirmative plan has better advantages than the counterplan. Attacking the net benefits is a defensive argument.

2. <u>Counterplan is procedurally unfair</u>: Counterplans are, in general, a fair negative strategy, but in specific cases the Negative oversteps its bounds. For example, the Affirmative might argue plan-inclusive counterplans are unfair. The Affirmative

needs to be specific about the problem in order to win a procedural argument.

3. Permutation: Show why a combination of the plan and counterplan (following permutation rules) is the superior option.

To recap how a permutation works:

SITUATION	WHO WINS?
CP alone is inferior to plan	Affirmative
CP alone is exactly as good as plan	Affirmative
CP alone is inferior to perm	Affirmative
CP alone is exactly as good as perm	Affirmative
CP alone is superior to both plan and perm	Negative

In order for the Negative to win the counterplan, it must prove that the counterplan <u>alone</u> is net beneficial to the plan alone and net beneficial to any legitimate permutations. In other words, ties go to the Affirmative. That is because the Negative must prove that there is an opportunity cost to the plan.

Please also remember that both non-intrinsic or severance permutations are unacceptable. If the Negative drops the counterplan, then the permutation goes away because a permutation is really just a test of the competitiveness of the counterplan. Continuing to advocate a permutation in the absence of a counterplan would also be non-intrinsic. On the other hand, if the Negative runs a counterplan, it does not give the Affirmative the right to abandon any part of its plan advocacy, which would be severance. All that the Affirmative should argue with a permutation is that the plan is still good and some part(s) of the counterplan might make it even better.

Review questions:

1. Compare and contrast agent and process counterplans.

2. What are the two different ways for counterplans to establish net benefits?

3. Explain arguments for and against: counterplan advocacy, counterplan conditionality, and counterplan dispositionality.

4. The topic, fiat limitations, and net benefits do not set limits on what counterplans can be argued successfully. Explain why.

5. Explain why competitiveness (or mutual exclusivity) sets the limit on what counterplans can be argued successfully. Your answer should include the term "permutation."

6. Explain arguments for and against the fairness of: PICs, severance permutations, and non-intrinsic permutations.

Milestone:

Analyze a plan versus counterplan match-up. Think about the net benefits the counterplan might claim. Also think about permutations the Affirmative might make. Is the counterplan strategically sound?

CHAPTER 10

Critiques

How are critiques different from counterplans?

A counterplan is a specific action that could be done instead of doing the plan. The Negative offers a concrete alternative, a different course of action. A critique, however, is the argument that the entire affirmative case is flawed, not because any one or two arguments are incorrect, but because the entire philosophy of the case is wrong.

A real-life example will make the distinction clear. Let's say our topic is *Resolved: We should eat pizza for dinner tonight.* The Affirmative offers a plan for going to Milano's restaurant and ordering a pepperoni and green pepper pizza and makes a persuasive case that this pizza is the most delicious food we could eat tonight. If the Negative responds that the Chinese food at Asian Grill is the most delicious food we could eat tonight, then it would be presenting a counterplan. If, however, the Negative responds that food choices should be based not on deliciousness but on healthfulness, then it would be presenting a critique. If the Negative goes on to say that we should go to Tofu Town vegetarian restaurant because it is more healthful, though admittedly less delicious, than Milano's pizza, then the Negative has presented a counterplan joined to a critique. A critique-counterplan combination can be a very powerful strategy, but for now, let's learn about the critique by itself, which is also a strong strategy.

The critique is an argument against the entire philosophy of the case. In our example, the Negative concedes that the plan does achieve its stated advantage: Milano's pizza is delicious. What the Negative contests is the importance of that goal. Sure, deliciousness is something we consider when selecting food, but it is not our only or even our most important consideration. Healthfulness, cost, and speediness are also relevant. Maybe we only have $20 and 30 minutes for dinner tonight; fast food might be the best option. The Affirmative presented a **framework** that deliciousness was the key consideration. A framework is the affirmative argument about how to evaluate and think about different kinds of advantages. (Look back to Chapter 6 for examples, the consequentialist and deontological frameworks.) A framework may be stated explicitly or merely implied, but it is always there. The Negative can win by conceding most of the case advantages but arguing that the framework is wrong.

Consider a critique in terms of the word "should." For example, the Affirmative might argue that "should" is best understood in general terms as a consequentialist philosophy of thinking about the ends rather than the means and in specific terms as a goal of maximizing tastiness. This interpretation of the word "should" links the case to the topic; under this framework, the case does affirm the topic in a prima facie way. But this is just one possible interpretation of "should." The word "should" could also be reasonably interpreted to mean maximizing a different consequentialist goal such as healthfulness. The word "should" could also be reasonably interpreted to mean following a deontological principle such as patronizing only locally owned restaurants, not chains or franchises. In other words, instead of an alternative action to the plan, a critique is an alternative interpretation of the word "should." The Negative offers an alternative framework.

All three interpretations of "should" in the preceding paragraph are reasonable because "should" is a blank slate. There is no single agreed-upon dictionary definition; "should" really expresses a mood of ought-ness rather than one specific philosophical idea. Remember how I said in Chapter 7 that certain words were ambiguous and thus made topics debatable? A critique is a debate over the merits of two different frameworks that interpret the ambiguous word in the topic, "should" or "ought" or "must" or whatever. This kind of critique is known as a **value critique**. The Negative is questioning—critiquing—the values that the Affirmative has used to support the topic. The Negative might be doing so from a variety of different perspectives, perhaps even from the standpoint that there are no universal values at all (relativism or even nihilism).

How are critiques similar to counterplans?

Critiques are very similar to counterplans in structural terms. Every structural idea that we just discussed for counterplans is also true for critiques but with slightly different names. Let's say the Negative argues a feminism critique, saying that the affirmative framework is based on masculine, not human, values. Let's look at the parts of this critique.

The most important part of the critique is the negative alternative framework, usually just called the **alternative** for short. In the feminist critique, the Negative is showing that "should" should not be understood from an exclusively masculine perspective. The alternative answers the question: what does the Negative propose instead of masculinist values? The negative alternative might be that, rather than obsessing over our duties (a masculine concept), we should instead consider caring and nurturing as most important (a more feminine concept). The Negative would then explain this in a text of the alternative. While the Affirmative does not usually provide a text of its framework, because the Negative is challenging the affirmative framework, the Negative must provide a text of its alternative. Rather than trying to write the text in their own words, Negatives sometimes quote famous philosophers. These writers sometimes use confusing rhetoric and complicated philosophical ideas, but whether you write your own or quote a philosopher, the text always serves the same function. It is the explanation of the Negative's view on how to understand philosophically which advantages are the most important to the topic.

Second, the Negative needs to show why the alternative is a better way to understand the topic than the affirmative framework. This argument is known as the **implication**; it is exactly analogous to the net benefits of a counterplan. The Negative might argue that feminist ethics are better, more consistent with the topic, or make for better debate rounds, for example: *Duty is boring, and a debate about nurturing is more educational.* Just like counterplans must be competitive, the implication must offer a reason to reject the case framework. Consider it this way: a plan could be good for more than one reason. For example, perhaps Milano's pizza is not only the most delicious but also the most healthful option. If this were true, then the Affirmative could concede the critique and still win. With the example of the feminist critique, if the Negative provides no reason to reject the case, then why choose? With frameworks, the idea of mutual exclusivity is crucial, for example: *Feminist ethics and masculinist ethics are incompatible.*

The critique also needs to show that the Affirmative actually uses the framework being critiqued. Remember that the affirmative framework is often implicit, rather than explicit. Worse, the Affirmative can switch frameworks because a plan could be good under both masculinist and feminist frameworks. Therefore, the Negative must pin the Affirmative down. It might argue that affirmative arguments lock the Affirmative into one framework, for example: *The clear masculinist ethics of the affirmative case means it cannot now take a feminist stance.* Or the Negative might argue that every topical affirmative case must use a certain framework to support the topic: *This topic requires a masculinist affirmative case.* It is not my view that policy topics do force a certain framework on the Affirmative; usually they are ambiguous. However, some judges do believe that some topics force a framework. Either way, the Negative needs to show a clear **link** between the affirmative case and its purported framework.

A lot of overly complicated hash is made of critiques, but that is all there to them. A critique is usually ordered: (a) link, (b) alternative, and (c) implication. The core argument of any value critique is: *Let's look at the topic in a better way.* The Negative shows that other considerations are more important than those the Affirmative has focused on.

Of course, some judges think critiques are unfair, believing that we ought to stick to whatever framework the Affirmative offers. Other judges believe that critiques lead to endless philosophical discussions that are irresolvable. They think that these questions, such as *Which way to interpret a topic is best?*, *What considerations are most important to making policy decisions?*, and *Should we use a consequentialist or deontological framework?* are inappropriate for policy debate. On the face of it, this makes some intuitive sense because these do seem like philosophical issues that are pointless to the broader policy question. However, if you think about it for a moment, you'll see how important critiques are. Why should the Affirmative have an unchallenged power to say what considerations matter most? This would give the Affirmative an unfair advantage to dictate the very terms of the debate. The Negative must at least be able to challenge the Affirmative if only to keep the Affirmative honest. Furthermore, philosophical questions are important to policy decisions. In the real world, policymakers ask questions about whether a goal is worthy or not and also about whether one goal is more important than another.

Are there any other types of critique?

Yes. There is also the logic or knowledge critique. These kinds of **epistemology critiques** (epistemology is the study of how we know for certain what we think we know) question whether the Affirmative has actually been able to prove anything at all. For example, one might argue on a domestic policy topic that all of the affirmative evidence is based on a flawed statistical research method; none of it is trustworthy for this reason. Or on a foreign policy topic, one might argue that the affirmative evidence is flawed because it is based on C.I.A. and military analysis that is biased and too likely to see threats everywhere, even where there are none. At their best, these epistemological critiques provide deep, thoughtful reasons to distrust the affirmative case. At their worst, this kind of critique is merely an "It's impossible to prove anything" argument (then why bother discussing anything?) or just a "Your author is dumb" indictment (often quoting a critic with questionable motives).

There are many critiques that straddle the line between value critiques and epistemology critiques, mixing elements of both. These critiques look for common causes of many separate problems. For example, the marxist critique links together analysis of several flaws of capitalist, free-market economic systems. This critique unites social problems (work-life imbalance and stress, declining marriage rates), cultural problems (violence in entertainment), environmental problems (climate change, pollution), and economic problems (unemployment, inflation, etc.) as having a root cause: capitalism. Partly, this is a value critique, arguing that capitalism is not a good system to pursue. But this is also an epistemology critique, arguing that researchers and writers tend to support economic systems that are in their best interests. In other words, the Affirmative's authors are capitalist stooges, if you put the argument in its most extreme form. The value plus epistemology critique can be quite powerful.

The marxist critique falls under **critical theory**. Critical theorists analyze how supposedly neutral or objective decision-making processes are, in fact, quite value-laden. For example, critical theorists argue that the judicial system does not operate fairly but is biased in favor of white people, the wealthy, and men. The mechanisms of bias can be nuanced and subtle or obvious and direct. That the wealthy can afford better lawyers is obvious and direct. That judges are often in the same social circles as the wealthy has more subtle effects. Critical theorists might also argue that policy analysis methods are biased to certain outcomes. Cost-benefit analysis, though an attempt to objectively forecast policy outcomes, might tend to recommend policies that benefit property owners but harm other people's less-quantifiable rights. Critical theory is an attempt to identify mechanisms of bias. When there is bias in some method of analysis, like cost-benefit analysis, or in some method of decision-making, like in the judicial system, then critical theory is operating like an epistemology critique. Unearthing hidden power structures and flawed worldviews is epistemological. But critical theory always combines this with a value critique by rejecting those power structures and worldviews.

Sometimes, these are known as **discourse critiques** if the theorists' emphasis is on the ways that official or professional speech—a discourse—is itself part of the power structure and helps create the worldview. Lawyers and judges' discourse keeps outsiders intimidated by the legal system, and it helps lawyers and judges feel more confident about legal decisions.

Discourse critiques should not be confused with the language "critique" in which a team is criticized for using offensive language. These are not, in fact, critiques. They are closer to procedural arguments about fair debate practices. I discuss them in Chapter 15.

Are there any good activities to practice critiques?

Yes. The best activity I know of is the "speaking in tongues" activity. Your coach posts several different philosophies you have studied at stations around the room, for example, *Feminism, Marxism,* and *Radical Environmentalism.* Each debater stands at a different station. The coach calls out an idea or policy, and each person gets two minutes to plan a 30-second speech. For example, the coach might say, "Nuclear-weapons-free zones," and then each debater would prepare his or her designated philosophy's take on that policy. The coach can decide whose speech best reflects his or her designated philosophy's perspective. Then every debater rotates to a different station, and the coach calls out a different idea or policy.

How does the Affirmative respond to critiques?

The Affirmative responds with many arguments that are similar to those it would use against a counterplan.

1. <u>No implication</u>: The Affirmative argues that the critique alternative is no better than the affirmative framework. This is analogous to the *No net benefit* argument against a counterplan. For example, the Affirmative might say that feminist ethics are not superior to masculinist ethics and therefore not a reason to reject the Affirmative.

2. <u>Critiques are procedurally unfair</u>: The Affirmative argues that the critique is unfair for debate and biases the debate. The Affirmative should specify clearly what problems the critique presents. For example, it might argue that critiques ask philosophical questions that cannot be answered in a short debate format.

3. <u>Permutation</u>: The Affirmative argues that the two frameworks are not mutually exclusive and that the case still affirms the topic even in the negative framework. For example, the plan might be moral under both masculinist and feminist ethics, or pizza might be both delicious and healthful. The Affirmative is showing with its permutation that the original framework and alternative framework are not in tension. The Affirmative proves that there is no opportunity cost to the case because the critique is not competitive. This is analogous to the permutation argument against a counterplan.

4. <u>No link</u>: The Affirmative can argue that it does not use the framework that the Negative says it does. If this can be shown to be true, it is a good defensive argument.

5. <u>Counter-critique</u>: While the critique is usually a negative position, the Affirmative can sometimes counter-critique the Negative, arguing that the alternative is morally suspect.

Review questions:

1. What are the similarities and differences of counterplans and critiques?

2. Define "framework," "alternative," "implication," and "link." Look at an example critique and analyze its structure in these terms.

3. What are some arguments for and against the critique as a reason to vote against the Affirmative?

4. Explain why competitiveness and permutations are arguments that also apply to critiques.

5. Explain how value and epistemology critiques are different. Give examples of each from the current topic.

6. Give arguments for and against the fairness of relativist and nihilist critiques.

Milestone:

Spend some time familiarizing yourself with the critiques you anticipate you might hear on the current topic. You ought to read some of the evidence, of course, but many critique authors write so densely that it is often better to read an introductory book about the author first. Strive to see through the complications and ask, "What is the value or logic that is being critiqued? Why? What is supposed to be wrong with it?"

CHAPTER 11

Disadvantages

Is a disadvantage related to an advantage?

Yes. A disadvantage is just the opposite of an advantage. Rather than something good that the plan causes, it is about something bad. All disadvantages have the same basic form, built on arguments about cause and effect. A basic disadvantage has at least three component parts: (1) link, *plan includes X*; (2) internal link, *X causes Y*; and (3) impact, *Y is bad.* Each part is important to understand.

Link

This is same argument as a critique link, except that a disadvantage link identifies what the plan does rather than what the framework is. It is an argument about how the plan could start this disadvantage, and it usually entails pointing to some specific plank or phrase in the plan text. Let's say we are debating a proliferation topic, *Resolved: The United States government should substantially increase pressure on nations seeking nuclear weapons.* Let's say that the Affirmative proposes military threats against Iran. The Negative might argue that there is a risk such threats spark war. The link stems directly from some plank in plan. What part of plan is the root cause of the problem? For example, perhaps the problem is that plan would threaten to use nuclear weapons in a first strike. The link is to point to plan text, *The Affirmative would not rule out the use of nuclear weapons*, and say that this could start the disadvantage.

Internal link

Now there must be a causal argument about how, given the link, the plan could lead to the final impact of war. As the Negative, you must argue for the steps, the **internal link(s)** of the disadvantage. This is exactly analogous to the solvency of an advantage on case. What would get us to war from a military threat? If we make threats, what happens next?

If U.S. makes threats → then Iranian hardliners gain power

So, what happens if they gain power?

If Iranian hardliners gain power → then Iran declares war on the U.S.

Now we've constructed a causal chain of internal links. A leads to B, B leads to C, etc., until we get to the impact. Each element in this chain is an internal link that must be proven.

Impact

So what? At the risk of sounding silly, who cares if there is a U.S.-Iran war? The argument that answers this question is the impact. It shows why the disadvantage is bad. Impacts are exactly analogous to the harm of an affirmative advantage. Furthermore, the disadvantage impact must outweigh (be more important than) any advantage harm:

Negative	Affirmative
Impact outweighs	· case harms
U.S.-Iran war	vs. stopping spread of nuclear weapons

If the impact doesn't outweigh the case harms, then there's no point to running the disadvantage, unless you can whittle the harms down to a point where the disadvantage does outweigh the advantages. Mixing case attacks and a disadvantage is a solid sword-and-shield approach. If the risk of the disadvantage outweighs picked-apart case harms, then the judge would vote for the disadvantage. It is all about weighing risks vs. benefits, also sometimes known as cost-benefit analysis.

So, how can a disadvantage outweigh an advantage? Well, there are three key factors in figuring out the risk: (a) magnitude, (b) probability, and (c) timeframe. The magnitude simply refers to the nastiness of the impact: war is a large magnitude impact. Destruction of the world's climate is an even larger magnitude impact. Probability refers to the likelihood of the impact. Is it a likely risk, say, 90%? Or is it a long-shot risk like 5%? Finally, **timeframe** refers to how long it will take the impact to come to fruition. War can happen quickly—even overnight. The destruction of the world's climate will take longer. It is a little silly to assign numbers to consequences that are difficult to quantify, but if you could, you would simply multiply/divide the three factors together to get the total:

Magnitude x Probability / Timeframe = Total impact

It seems simple. Is there anything else to it?

If you are arguing for a **linear** disadvantage, no. Linear disadvantages explain how the plan gradually, incrementally incurs problems. For example, a linear disadvantage might argue that *Each dollar we spend on the plan reduces the government's ability to pay for vital social services, harming the poorest people.* If the plan spends $20 million, then 900 people would be hurt. If the plan spends $40 million, then 1,800 people would be hurt. However, the disadvantage about the plan causing a war with Iran is not linear. Either there will be a war, or not.

This idea of an extreme catastrophe is known as a brink-based disadvantage. A **brink** is the argument that the disadvantage is just about to happen and any small change could push us over the edge. The brink is also sometimes called a **threshold**. We are right now on the edge of a cliff. For example, the U.S. relationship with Iran is tense right now, and even a small thing—like an affirmative plan that threatens to use nuclear weapons—could push things over the edge. The brink-based disadvantage is a risk analysis (unlikely but large magnitude impact); the linear disadvantage is an incremental analysis (near certain but small magnitude impact). In a linear disadvantage, the argument is that the plan will only make bad problems worse. In a brink-based disadvantage, the argument is not that things are already bad, only that they are on the edge of catastrophe.

For each and every brink, the Negative must be able to show than no other cause will initiate that step. Think of our model that A causes B, B causes C, and so on. What if B just happened on its own in the status quo? Then we still might get to the impact, even without the plan. It may seem odd to say, but if there is going to be war with Iran whatever the U.S. does, then at least the judge can choose to minimize the case harms.

To argue a brink-based disadvantage, you need to be able to prove that every causal argument is unique: that it won't happen in the status quo, that it would only happen if the plan happens. Alternatively, if the Negative is running a counterplan, then it needs to prove that the counterplan would not cause the disadvantage. This argument about the status quo or counterplan avoiding the disadvantage is known as **uniqueness**. Of course, uniqueness also applies to advantages: the Affirmative wants to show that the advantage is a unique benefit to doing the plan that the status quo or a counterplan would not capture. However, no one refers to this as uniqueness; they just make the argument.

Many debaters use the terms brink and uniqueness interchangeably, but they are different. The brink is the *We're on the edge of catastrophe* argument; the uniqueness is the *compared my opponent's option* argument.

Are brink-based disadvantages more powerful?

They are. Unfortunately, they are more complicated. When you start to think about brinks, you realize the simple picture we painted before of the internal links, A → B → C, is not quite accurate. It contains a mistake known as the slippery slope fallacy. It is too much of an oversimplification. A alone doesn't cause B to happen. Try this thought experiment: imagine a pencil balanced on a finger. Eventually, the wind always blows it over, but it was in an unstable position. Was the wind the cause, or was it being balanced on a finger? The wind gust that blows the pencil over is the proximate cause of its fall, while the underlying instability of the finger-balanced position is the structural cause.

Internal links are arguments about proximate causes, but we assume the conditions, or structural causes, were already in place. If the U.S. were to threaten Iran, that alone isn't going to cause Iran to declare war on the U.S. Several other things must be true. For example, the hardliners would need to be strong. If they were weak, threats might never result in retaliation. Also, moderate Iranian politicians would have to be weak. So, our diagram should look more like this:

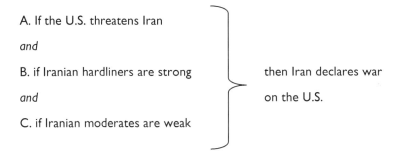

A. If the U.S. threatens Iran

and

B. if Iranian hardliners are strong   then Iran declares war

and   on the U.S.

C. if Iranian moderates are weak

Each thing is necessary to cause the next step but not sufficient on its own. In other words, at least three factors need to be true for Iran to declare war on the U.S. What would happen if the U.S. threatened Canada? There are no military hardliners in power currently; there would be no North American war.

We also know that for the impact to happen, certain things cannot be the case. For example, if the U.S. threatens Iran, but Iran's political system collapses, then there would be no war.

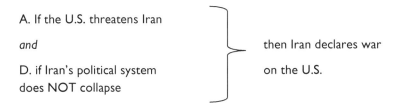

A. If the U.S. threatens Iran

and   then Iran declares war

D. if Iran's political system   on the U.S.
does NOT collapse

Causality arguments are tricky because so many factors, both contributing and restraining, must be lined up properly for the internal link chain to happen. We can simplify all the above conditions into an Ishikawa diagram with all the contributing factors

(A, B, C) like weak moderates above the main line and restraining factors (D, E, F) like a strong political system below the main line:

internal links

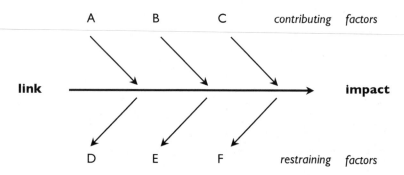

This diagram corrects the slippery slope fallacy. The causal chain of the internal links would happen only in certain, specified conditions.

How does the Affirmative respond to a disadvantage?

There are ten different arguments that an Affirmative can use against a disadvantage. They are grouped into three main types.

1. Attack the uniqueness:

    a. Non-unique: The status quo or counterplan is as likely as the plan to cause the disadvantage. If neither policy is comparatively better at avoiding the risk, then the disadvantage is a moot point.

    b. Alternate causality: Another cause unrelated to this plan will inevitably lead to the disadvantage, making it a moot point. This alternate cause could enter at any point along the causal chain of the disadvantage. Technically, this is exactly the same argument as a non-unique, but "alternate causality" is used more broadly. *Counterplan spends money too, causing economic collapse* is a non-unique; *Russia is going to trigger oil shocks, causing economic collapse* is an alternate causality.

2. Attack the link:

   a. <u>No link</u>: The plan does not actually do what the Negative says would start the disadvantage.

   b. <u>Empirically denied</u>: A historical example should have but did not cause the disadvantage, so it must be a false risk.

   c. <u>No brink</u> (or <u>No threshold</u>): There is no specified tipping point, or the tipping point is not proven. A closely related argument is that the plan is not enough to push things over the brink to cause the disadvantage. This is often phrased as <u>Uniqueness overwhelms the brink</u> or <u>Uniqueness overwhelms the link</u>: the status quo is so stable that the risk of the disadvantage is nil. Basically, these arguments show that the disadvantage is impossible by granting the disadvantage's uniqueness.

   d. <u>Link turn</u>: The plan would prevent the disadvantage. If you turn the link, you also want a non-unique argument; that way, the plan has a comparative advantage over the status quo or counterplan.

3. Attack the impact:

   a. <u>No internal link</u> (or <u>Non-intrinsic</u>): Even if the disadvantage begins, reaching the impact is too improbable. Every internal link unrealistically assumes that future events are entirely predictable. In other words, the cause-and-effect chain will break down because future policymakers will act unpredictably to prevent calamity. This is an argument about the improbability of the impact.

   b. <u>No timeframe</u>: The impact is too far in the future to matter.

   c. <u>No impact</u>: The impact is not so bad or is nonexistent. This is often coupled with the argument that <u>Case outweighs</u>: the case advantages are bigger than the impact.

   d. <u>Impact turn</u>: Explain why the impact would actually be good, not bad. Note: Do not make this with a link turn!

A link turn plus an impact turn results in a **double-turn**. You certainly should never argue that the plan prevents something good!

Review questions:

1. What is the difference between a link and an internal link?

2. How is the total impact of a disadvantage measured? Give examples of disadvantages that do not have a big impact in three distinct ways.

3. Define "brink" and "threshold." What is the difference between a linear and a brink-based disadvantage?

4. Define "uniqueness" and "slippery slope fallacy." Why is it important for each causal step to have uniqueness?

5. Why should a link turn be accompanied by a non-unique argument? Give an example.

6. What is a double-turn? Give an example. Why is it bad?

Milestone:

Make a comprehensive list of all the cases on the current topic. Then, decide which generic disadvantages work best against each case. Your goal should be to have at least one but preferably two disadvantages ready against every case.

What is a procedural argument?

Every debate has two components: the procedural debate and the substantive debate. Procedural arguments are your response when your opponent does something unfair. They are usually about your opponent's advocacy. Both sides need to have a chance in the game, which means that the judge must <u>always</u> resolve any procedural arguments first <u>before</u> looking to substantive ones. Unfair opponent advocacy can skew and distort the substantive ground.

> Procedural arguments always take precedence
> OVER substantive arguments.

Sometimes debaters say that procedural arguments are **a priori**: the judge decides them before (or prior to) looking to the substantive debate. Of course, you never win just for being fair. All you can do is beat back an accusation of unfairness; this means that it is a risk-less strategy for the accuser. Procedural arguments are referred to as debate theory. This book, specifically Chapters 6 to 12, is about debate theory.

Usually, procedural attacks are made by the Negative against the Affirmative. This is because Affirmatives have the power of parametrics, which means that the Affirmative is usually the one whose advocacy is unfair. But not always. The Negative can lose, too, for unfairness. However, the most common procedural attacks are negative attacks on plan topicality and, to a lesser extent, affirmative fiat abuse.

How do I write a procedural argument?

Procedural arguments are quite similar in structure to disadvantages. It is useful to think of them as disadvantages that link to your opponents' advocacy: *My opponent advocates X type of argument, X arguments cause Y kind of debate*, and *Y debate is bad*. This is how to structure any procedural argument. First, you need to prove what your opponent advocates (or fails to advocate). Second, you need to prove that this advocacy changes the way the debate round evolves. Third, you need to prove that this change is bad.

Let's look at an example, an attack on topicality. First, topicality attacks begin with an interpretation where the Negative explains how it interprets the topic. This might include the definition(s) of some key word(s) in the topic. In essence, the Negative begins its attack by contradicting the affirmative interpretation.

This is followed by the **violation** that explains why the affirmative plan does not meet the Negative's interpretation. In other words, the Negative is establishing the link, the same as it does on a critique or disadvantage. In any other procedural argument, the violation would also be the first argument: *The affirmative framework text is irrelevant, The counterplan text is vague, My opponent lied in cross-examination, The plan abuses fiat*, etc. The interpretation and violation are flip sides of the same coin: what the topic should mean and what the Affirmative has twisted it to mean.

The third argument is what consequences this has for a debate round's evolution. This is the internal link of a topicality attack. It is known as the **standards**. What kind of debate would allowing this kind of violation lead to? You might argue that *Non-topical plans lead to unpredictable debates* or *Non-topical plans lead to unrealistic debates*. A standard is therefore a hypothesis about what the world of debate would look like if whatever behavior identified in the violation were allowed to fly in every round.

However, remember that, just like with any disadvantage, there must also be uniqueness. It is not enough to show that your opponent's advocacy leads to bad debate; you must also show that your stance would lead to <u>better</u> debate. So, standards arguments are really two-fold: they show that the advocacy you attack in the violation leads to bad debate rounds, and they also show that the advocacy you propose in the interpretation would lead to good debate rounds. For example, you might argue that *Topical plans lead to more meaningful rounds.*

The final part of a topicality argument is the voting issue, or simply, the **voter**. This is the impact argument. So what if the affirmative plan makes debate unpredictable? Well, it matters because predictability is important to good debate, for example: *Unpredictable debate rounds skew everyone's strategic choices.* If you stop and think about it this way, you'll realize a few important things about any procedural argument. Just as with a regular disadvantage, procedural impacts must be persuasive to the judge. For example, predictability is an important goal for debate, but you need to explain to the judge why unpredictability is an impact worth avoiding. How is it bad, specifically? Just as with disadvantage impacts, procedural impacts must be compelling. The only difference is that disadvantage impacts are about the real world, whereas procedural impacts are about the game of debate competition.

Furthermore, you should also realize that procedural impacts can be weighed against each other. What if the U.S. Congress just voted down an amendment yesterday and the affirmative plan is to pass it? In this instance, maybe some unpredictability is less important than how realistic the example is. Furthermore, one procedural attack could also have multiple procedural impacts—topicality can be a voting issue for many distinct reasons—all of which you can bring up in one round. This allows you to hit multiple impacts, and one of them might be more persuasive to your judge. If you can establish a convincing procedural impact to a topicality attack, then you have established the voting issue.

This is all there is to any kind of procedural argument: interpretation and violation, standards, and voting issue.

How do I prove that the affirmative plan does not meet the topic?

Let's take an example topicality from the pollution topic, *Resolved: That the United States government should reduce worldwide pollution through its trade and/or aid policies.* One plan on this topic was to fiat that the U.S. government should sign the Basel Convention, which would prohibit the trade of hazardous materials between countries. Amazingly, many poor nations accept payment from rich nations to dump toxic waste in their countries.

The Negative begins its topicality attack with a definition of the relevant word(s) in the topic. Dictionary definitions are fine; definitions from expert authors and journals are better because they are more specific. Expert definitions are also known as contextual definitions. "Common man" definitions, such as definitions you might find in a newspaper, are also fine. You don't necessarily even need a published source. If you can write a clear, fair definition, which lucidly articulates what the topic should mean, then your own definition might be sufficient.

A.   Definition from *Russell's Dictionary*, 2014:

Pollution – (noun) 1. the act of releasing dangerous or harmful materials into the general surroundings, environment, or system; 2. the materials so released

The next part is the violation. The violation is simply an explanation of why you think the affirmative plan is not within the topic as you've defined it:

B.   Violation:

Basel would apply to materials that are being moved between nations for proper disposal, although some nations fail to follow the rules. Proper disposal of hazardous material isn't pollution. Therefore, the affirmative plan does not meet the word "pollution" in the topic.

Understand? The argument is that the trade of hazardous waste isn't pollution. It's what the recipient countries might do with the waste that's pollution, but the plan doesn't affect that.

The next part is the standards, which explain why the Affirmative's advocacy is bad. Many debaters will never change their standards and give the same vague explanation of each standard. These multi-purpose, multi-use standards are meaningless and useless. The point is to give an argument about what precedents this specific Affirmative is setting, so standards really do need to change for every topicality attack. Here are three examples:

C. Standards:

1. **Framers' intent**: The topic intends for the Affirmative to use U.S. trade and/or aid policies as the mechanism to reduce pollution. The Affirmative instead treats trade itself as a form of pollution. For example, why not require more experienced ship captains to reduce oil spills, tankers to run on solar power, or ship-hull disinfections to keep invasive species from migrating?

2. **Limits**: Restricting the Affirmative to plans that prohibit international pollution is an important way to reduce our research burden and allow for more in-depth debate.

3. **Plans that meet our interpretation**: ban pesticide sales; require catalytic converters on cars sold to South America and Asia; give development aid to poor countries in return for protection of forests; or build nuclear reactors in China to reduce coal-power electricity.

The first two are cogent arguments for why your interpretation of the topic is reasonable and leads to good debate. The third standard, what plans meet your interpretation, should always be included in the standards. Always give examples of what's fair.

Now we can move on to the voting issues. Let's look at a couple on the same topicality attack against Basel.

D. Voting issues:

1. **Fairness**: The Affirmative gained an unfair advantage by being non-topical. Unfair debates are bad because both teams should have equal ground to advocate.

    a. **In-round abuse**: Real anti-pollution policies are unpopular because they limit the daily pollution allowed to businesses, hurting the economy and decreasing jobs. The Affirmative presents a safety policy, which is popular. The Affirmative therefore "spikes" out of our politics disadvantage. The division of arguments in this round is unfair.

b. **Potential abuse**: Even if the Affirmative has not gained an unfair advantage in this round, their interpretation could be used to gain an unfair advantage in a later round. They might even go on to run some more ridiculous plan. If we hypothetically accepted the Affirmative's rationale for all the rounds this year, it would lead to bad debates. The division of all arguments on this topic (even those not mentioned in this round) is unfair.

2. **Education**: The Affirmative makes this round uneducational, which is bad.

    a. **Depth v. breadth**: Depth is better for the education value of debate than breadth [or vice-versa].

    b. **Wrong subject**: We should be learning about anti-pollution, not safety, policies.

There are many other tacks you can take with voting issues—all you have to do is identify what your opponent "does" to debate, and then make an impact about it—but fairness and education are two very common voting issues.

Remember that topicality is a voting issue in policy debate because the Affirmative advocates its plan. If the plan fails to be a valid defense of this topic because it, in effect, affirms a different topic, then the judge has no right to vote for the Affirmative because the Affirmative hasn't played its role. This is known as the **jurisdiction** voting issue. In this view, the judge is like a Supreme Court justice who can only uphold or overturn the law at hand and should not make decisions on any issues he or she sees fit to, which would be out of bounds.

What about fiat abuse?

The structure is the same as any other procedural argument: make a clear link to the affirmative advocacy (point to the plan text), explain standards of what fiat abuse causes (for example, the Affirmative could come up with unrealistic options that are impossible to predict), and finish with voting issues explaining why this is bad. That's all there is to it.

What about affirmative procedural attacks on the Negative?

There's no difference. The structure is exactly the same.

How do I answer a topicality attack or any other procedural argument?

Basically, the accused has four responses it can make to any procedural argument, and it should always try to make all four:

1. <u>Plan meets interpretation</u>: Explain how you don't actually commit whatever your opponent believes to be a problem. This is also sometimes called <u>No violation</u>. It is analogous to a *No link* argument in response to a disadvantage. Alternatively, you can also show that your opponent is just as guilty of the same sin, like a *Non-unique*. Of course, this only works in a very few situations!

2. <u>Interpretation</u> or <u>Violation is bad</u>: Explain why your opponent's interpretation, what he or she wants you to advocate, would be worse for debate than your actual advocacy. This is like a *Link turn* against a disadvantage.

3. <u>No voting issue</u>: Explain why you feel that you should not lose the round, even if your advocacy is deemed unfair.

   a. Even if you do change debate as your opponent claims you do, <u>the specified procedural impact is not bad</u>. This is like a *No impact* argument against a disadvantage.

   b. Even if you make the debate less fair for your opponent, <u>the substantive debate is more important</u>. This is the argument that procedurals should never be voting issues. This hardly ever flies, but it might work if the procedural debate is really muddy. This is why it's often coupled with the argument that procedural issues are impossible to adjudicate.

c. Even if you do change debate as your opponent claims
you do, <u>the specified impact is actually good for debate</u>.
This is like an *Impact turn* against a disadvantage.

You can make multiple arguments for each type of response.
There's one final kind of response that you can make to procedural arguments:

4. <u>Counter-interpretation</u>: Explain an alternative or re-explain
your original vision of what you think a fair debate round
should look like, explain why you meet that vision, and then
explain why your counter-interpretation creates the best possible debate. This is also known as <u>Counter-standards</u>.

A **counter-interpretation** is one of the most powerful responses to
a procedural argument, but it must have all three parts listed to
work. It's the only way for the accused to go on the offensive. A
counter-interpretation provides an alternative to the attacker's
interpretation:

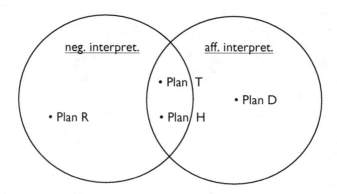

Let's say that the Affirmative is running plan D. The two sides
agree that plans T and H are fair; they disagree about plans R and
D. Now we have an argument about which interpretation would
be best for all debates on this topic. Would it be better to debate
the set of plans the Negative proposes {T, R, H} or the Affirmative
set of plans {H, T, D} for every round? The judge will vote for the
interpretation that makes for the best possible world of debate.

To make a decision about which interpretation is best, the
judge will listen carefully to the arguments both sides present. Ul-

timately, that is what every procedural debate is about: what is best for debate—not just for this round but as a principle for all rounds. Of course, the judge might vote for predictability in one round and against it in the next, but the judge is in both instances considering arguments about what effects predictability has on all rounds.

Review questions:

1. Explain the differences and similarities between procedural arguments and disadvantages.

2. Define "interpretation," "violation," "standards," and "voting issue."

3. What are the key factors of a good definition?

4. Explain why a good interpretation must clearly and fairly separate cases into topical and non-topical grounds.

5. Explain the competing interpretation view of a definition versus counter-definition debate.

6. Why are procedural arguments a priori? Give some arguments for and against the fairness, education, and jurisdiction voting issues.

Milestone:

There are not many good topicality arguments on a given topic. Discuss the merits of every topicality argument on the current topic with your teammates. Which topicality attacks can be used against what cases?

Rhetoric

He who knows only his own side of the case, knows little of that. Nor is it enough that he should hear the arguments of adversaries from his own teachers. He must be able to hear them from persons... who defend them in earnest. He must know them in their most plausible and persuasive form.

~ John Stuart Mill, *On Liberty*, 1859

I know all of the relevant theories for affirming and negating, and I know about my topic. Am I ready to compete in debate?

Almost. Before you begin competing, you need to practice, and no one can help you more than your teammates. You need a lot of practice and preparation before you are ready to compete. No one can do all the preparation on his or her own. It's important that you share ideas, strategies, and research duties with your teammates. It is also crucial that you have as many practice rounds as possible, especially in your first year, but also for your entire debate career.

I have a few recommendations for maximizing what you get out of your practice rounds:

1. Participate <u>regularly</u>; you wouldn't exercise sporadically.

2. Be prepared for each practice round. Disclose your arguments to your "opponent" so that the practice round will be as challenging as possible.

3. Try to compete against all different ability levels on your team, from beginners like yourself to advanced debaters. Maybe your coach would even be willing to take you on.

4. Try cutting down your preparation time during the round to make things more challenging. Alternatively, try increasing preparation time but use that time to predict what you think your opponent is about to do. This kind of pause-and-reflect practice helps develop strategic thinking.

5. Ask your coach to try a "start-stop" practice round where he or she gives feedback every 30 seconds, followed by a do-over.

6. Ask your teammates to each write you a ballot or give you an oral critique. Getting feedback from multiple perspectives helps.

7. Redo your rebuttal for homework.

8. If you are observing a practice round, you need to flow.

Right now, you're inexperienced, so you'll be relying on your more experienced teammates as a source of knowledge about techniques, skills, and so on. Just like your coach, they are also your teachers, which means that you need to show them respect. When you are just a beginner, you support the team by playing by the rules; when you have more experience, you will support the team by taking on a leadership role to teach the new beginners. Don't look on this as a burden, though. Teaching others is one of the best ways to continue developing your skills and to enrich your own knowledge.

The biggest problem with practice rounds is that they can be boring and repetitive. Therefore, it is best if one of the sides agrees to be the "dummy" (usually the more advanced team). The dummy half-acts, by pretending to be an opponent team in style and substance, but also tries to win. The dummy team uses the case or positions of some opponent you might face. This keeps the process of practice from becoming stale and predictable.

What exactly do you mean by style?

There are four basic opponent styles you'll face:

1. Spreaders
2. Hedgehogs
3. Entrappers
4. Persuaders

The first type of opponents you'll face are spreaders: they are fast and not afraid to use it. They will likely bring up many, many issues, and then kick out of most of them. It's likely you'll barely have time to put one or two refutations on each issue after their first speech, and then they will kick down to one issue and spend all their time, with considerable speed, on those one or two refutations you managed to get out. In other words, they're trying to squeeze your time and make you drop arguments. For this reason, it is vital that you cover. The best way to do this is to make sure that the one or two refutations you get out on each issue are the best answers you have. This is why you should write blocks with the best answers first. In fact, you can sometimes reverse the time pressure and put it back on them, if your arguments make it difficult for them to narrow down. They can be intimidating when they first stand up to speak and start putting out a dozen issues. Just keep your cool, prioritize, stay organized, and cover!

The second type of opponents you might face are the hedgehogs: they know one thing and know it well. They are likely to bring up only this one issue in their first speech, and they will spend nearly all their time developing it. They'll be able to predict your answers before you even make them. These hedgehogs attain their expertise on this one issue by knowing little about anything else. Try making as many connections between their pet issue and your favorite issues. The key is to push them away from their issue onto terrain you choose. You will have a tough time out-smarting them on their home turf; your best chance is to bring them to yours. The constant tension in debate is between depth versus breadth of preparation, and the hedgehogs don't have breadth. (By the way, those that know a little about a lot of topics are known as foxes and survive on their cleverness and adaptability.)

The third type of opponents you'll encounter are the entrappers: they will set you up to make one ghastly strategic mistake. For example, they will often make an argument that invites a certain logical response from you. Be careful! If the answer seems very obvious, ask yourself, will this argument get me into trouble in the whole debate? The entrappers rely upon you being focused too much on the line-by-line and not paying enough attention to the whole round. The best way to beat entrappers is by not walking into the trap! A subtype you might encounter are the theorizers: they are willing to have extensive debates about procedural issues, about what kinds of arguments are acceptable, and are waiting for you to make "unfair" arguments. Again, don't fall into their trap. You'll regret it if you do. In a way, entrappers are like especially tricky hedgehogs.

The fourth type of opponents you'll face are the persuaders: they will often completely ignore the line-by-line—sometimes even lie—and instead give the judge persuasive overviews. The worst mistake here is for you to ignore the line-by-line and go only to their overviews. Persuaders have practiced using clever turns of phrase and powerful rhetoric to make their arguments seem more powerful. You need to be disciplined. Stick to the line-by-line, go through and extend every argument you're winning, and then sum it all up with good overviews. If you lack this discipline, then you'll let the debate be entirely about rhetorical persuasion, and the persuaders are prepared to beat you in that game.

Being cordial to your opponents is tough because they are trying to beat you, and these behaviors can be irritating—but they feel that way because each type is an extreme example of certain valuable skills. The best debaters have mastered all of the skills, and so are balanced: persuasive, clever, well prepared, and efficient on the line-by-line, all in one round. The best debaters of all are a composite of the four types and have no real weaknesses. Knowing what to expect from each style because you've seen it in a practice round can help you keep your cool and focus on the arguments of your opponents rather than getting frustrated and making an *ad hominem*, or personal, attack.

There is another reason why having someone be the dummy team in practice rounds is so important: it will force you to practice all of your skills, so that you do not turn into a debater with a lop-sided skill set (good on persuasion, short on expertise; or vice versa). Being the dummy, or debating against the dummy, will push you to develop all your skills.

What are differences between a practice round and competition?

Not many. In fact, I recommend that you think of a competition round as a practice round with consequences: you're always learning, and you always want to do the best that you can, but it is best to keep it in proper perspective. Furthermore, the debate community takes good sportsmanship quite seriously, and while competitiveness is acceptable within the round, it should be set aside after the round. After all, opponents are often your friends from other schools. I have even seen teams share research with their opponents before the round begins. This is supposed to be an educational activity, so outright displays of aggression are frowned upon. Win or lose, having a good round is more important than being a cutthroat competitor.

For the same reason, judges also act a lot like your coach does during a practice round. Many judges will tell you their decision, explain it, and even answer questions after the debate is over. This is known as an oral critique. Some judges do not want or like to do this (some tournaments even have rules against oral critiques), instead preferring to write their decision and reasons down on their ballot, which you'll get back at the end of the tournament. Whether they give written or oral feedback, you should treat your judges respectfully because they are trying to help you improve. There will be more about adapting to your judge in Chapter 15.

The only two major differences between practice rounds and real competition rounds are the potentials for greater intra-partnership tension and running out of preparation time. These both stem from the excitement of actual competition: you want to win, so you push your partner too hard (or vice versa). You want to win, so you lose focus and don't manage your prep time carefully. I'll address how to reduce both of these sources of anxiety through practice.

There are good ways and bad ways to work with a partner?

Yes. Interacting with your partner can be both fun and difficult at times, but you can make it easier or harder on yourself. Sometimes, you may disagree. Underneath it all, I bet your partner is a reasonable human being. The key is to try to be open and honest with your partner. Don't blame him or her for every mistake—we often blame others most strongly when we know it is really us who is at fault—but don't hide your own sentiments just to protect your partner's feelings. If you follow this simple principle of "fair honesty" and can admit your own faults and also gently discuss your partner's, then I believe you will have a loyal, successful partnership. If you just can't seem to work together, talk to your coach or teacher.

What happens if your partner forgets something during his or her speech? Can you interrupt and say it for them? No. No one wants you to give your partner's speech, and only the words said by the designated speaker will be flowed. The judge ignores everything else. Plus, you've now alienated your partner. However, for some judges, it is acceptable to **prompt** your partner, that is, to jog his or her memory, but for others it is not. If you can prompt, the best technique is to ask your partner a relevant question. For example, if your partner is about to forget to answer the opponent's argument Z, ask, "What do you say about Z?" This works well because everyone has an easy time answering questions. The worst way to prompt is to write your refutation to argument Z on paper and give it to your partner. We understand someone else's refutation very slowly and read their handwriting even more slowly, and your partner will lose valuable speech time.

Finally, remember that in every debate, the last speech is the most important, so the first speaker has to provide whatever setup the second speaker wants. A struggle over who's in control is probably the single biggest source of partner tension, yet there's a clear answer: the final rebuttalist is the boss. That's why I always advise my teams to divide responsibilities for final rebuttals by side: one debater is the first affirmative and the second negative speaker (1A/2N); the other debater is the 2A/1N. That way, one partner bears the primary responsibility for the affirmative rounds, and the other partner bears the primary responsibility for the negative rounds. Neither partner bears all the responsibility for every round.

The other big source of partner tension is preparation time. It is important that plenty of preparation time is saved for the final rebuttal.

I never seem to have enough preparation time in practice rounds, and I'm guessing it'll be even harder in actual competition. What can I do about it? How do you "practice" preparation time?

Managing your **prep time**, or down time, well is crucial to winning close debates, and it is a difficult skill to master. The total amount is determined by the tournament, but how you allocate it is up to you. The only stipulation is that you can't use your prep

time during the middle of your speeches or during your opponent's speeches. It is also important to realize that in every kind of
debate, there is "virtual" or unofficial prep time. Being a good
manager of your prep time means knowing these hidden caches of
time and maximizing the use of your official time. There are four
basic considerations.

First, prep time is not for you to write out all your arguments
word-for-word, or worse, write them out for your partner. Good
debaters have their most important arguments pre-blocked or pre-
briefed before the round begins. If you find yourself consistently
running out of prep time during rounds, you might need to prepare more beforehand. Once the round starts, what happens if
you don't have a block? Do you write out a new block during
prep time? There is probably not enough time to do that even at
the most prep-time generous tournaments, so just wing it, and
write the block first thing at the end of the debate.

The second consideration is how to use prep time during a
round. Again, it's not for writing out your speech word-for-word.
Instead, prep time allows you to collect your thoughts and plan
your overall strategy. It is a time to confer with your partner or to
think quietly by yourself. When you use it to write notes for your
or your partner's speech, I recommend the one-word mnemonic
device. On your flow, write down one word in the appropriate
place to remind you of the argument you want to make. For example, your opponent argues that the economy is performing
poorly. You write down: *house, dollar,* and then *stocks. House* reminds you to argue *The housing market is doing well; dollar* reminds
you to argue *The dollar is strong;* and *stocks* reminds you to argue *The
stock market has slowed but has not stopped growing.* One-word mne-
monics are incredibly effective in triggering your memory. In this
way, you can plan out your entire speech by writing only 50 or 60
or 100 words. In other words, your speech is extemporaneous in
its delivery but planned in its argumentation. Learning this technique is a skill that you can and should develop in practice
rounds.

Third, you must consider prep time strategically. Take prep
time if you need it: a debate round can become complex quickly,
and taking a moment to ensure that you aren't painting yourself
into a corner is often critical. However, you need to consider your
prep time allocation as whole. If you are extremely well prepared
before the round even begins, you can minimize your down time

before your constructive speeches and first rebuttal and reserve almost all of it for your final rebuttal. If properly executed, this can lead to devastatingly clear final rebuttals, allowing you time to clarify the round in your mind before speaking. What is important in a debate is the final rebuttal, the persuasive part that really sells the judge. Practice with limited time to help improve your awareness of time used.

Fourth, you can gain "virtual" prep time by flowing your opponent's speech while simultaneously prepping. Sometimes, your opponent may be yammering on without making any arguments such that you have an extra second here and there to use the one-word mnemonic technique. Of course, be careful! The highest priority is to have a good flow: virtual prep time is meaningless if you miss an opponent's argument. If you have a partner you really trust, you can share a flow—but I recommend against this.

Another cache of virtual prep time is your opponent's prep time. Every time he's prepping, you should be too. The best way to use your opponent's prep time is to begin working on your final rebuttal summary. Yes, even at the beginning of the debate! This allows you to keep an eye focused on how you want the debate to end. Even if you have to keep reworking your overview, it's still helpful for your strategic clarity. Both of these techniques (prepping as you flow, pre-writing the final rebuttal) can be practiced in a practice round.

Finally, there is always pre-round prep time. Tournaments have a lot of free time, so you can get a lot done in between rounds. If you find out that an opponent school has a new argument or position or case, then start brainstorming your answers, rather than sitting around playing cards or listening to music. Pre-tournament, though, is the greatest cache of virtual prep time. You have hours, days, weeks, or months to ready yourself. Use it wisely!

I've heard some of my teammates talk about going to camp over the summer. Does it help?

It can! Many college debate teams host summer debate camps, where you can research your topics, get pointers on researching, and have multiple practice debates. If you take camp seriously, think hard about your topic, and improve from your camp practice rounds, then camp can be the best way to start the year!

Review questions:

1. What types of opponents will you face? Describe each type's strengths and weaknesses.

2. Why should you be friendly and respectful to your opponents and judges?

3. How can you get the most benefit from practice rounds? from competition rounds?

4. What do you need to do to work with a partner successfully?

5. On a debate team, who is the boss?

6. Name the five different techniques to manage prep time, and explain how to use each one.

Milestone:

You should be practicing regularly and getting ready for your first tournament!

CHAPTER 14

Competing

What are competitions like? Whom do I compete against?

Most debaters are cool people, and debate competitions end up being a lot of fun. If you enjoy your debate class or club, then you ought to try competing at a tournament at least once. If you're thinking about competing, I would reading recommend Gary Alan Fine's scholarly book *Gifted Tongues* (Princeton University Press, 2001) or Joe Miller's journalistic book *Cross-X* (Farrar, Straus and Giroux, 2006) as ways to learn more about competitions—or just go to one.

Whether you debate only in your classroom or pursue inter-scholastic competition at **tournaments**, the ideas, concepts, and skills are exactly the same. Before we discuss tournament specifics, it's important to note that because your school sponsors you to go to a tournament, it's considered a school event, and therefore all the usual school rules apply.

A tournament consists of teams from several schools that travel to the host school for the competition, which usually occurs on a weekend. There is considerable variation in tournament size. Some tournaments have fewer than a half-dozen schools; some tournaments have hundreds of schools. The coaches who attend form the judging pool and judge the debates, but of course coaches never judge their own students.

Many tournaments will offer more than one kind of debate, and within each kind of debate, there will usually be divisions by experience. Thus, one single tournament might have a dozen divisions of debate going on simultaneously. You compete only against people with roughly the same experience level as you. There is almost always a novice division (beginners in their first year of debate), which means that you would first compete against beginners just like yourself. Often, there is an intermediate division, sometimes called junior varsity. And there is always an uppermost division for the most experienced debaters, usually called varsity (sometimes called champion, open, or senior).

How long do tournaments last?

Tournaments can vary between two to twenty rounds of competition. Twenty rounds takes multiple days to complete. For this reason, some tournaments take entire weekends, while short two to five round tournaments may take only a day. Every debater will switch sides several times: you'll be on each side for half of your rounds. Tournaments assign your opponents for each round and usually your side as well. If there are an uneven number of debate teams in a division, one team will be assigned a **bye**, a debate-less win. You will never get two byes at one tournament. Before each round is set to begin, the tournament will post a list of who's debating whom in what room. This list is called a posting, pairing, or sometimes a schematic. You may be listed by name or by a code, so check the pairings carefully.

Most tournaments have two types of rounds: preliminary and elimination. **Preliminary** rounds are guaranteed for everyone at the tournament, and if you lose, you still have more debates to follow. Everyone competes in every preliminary round. After all the preliminary rounds are over, the debaters with the best records advance to the next stage, the elimination rounds, where sides are often determined by coin flips. In the elimination phase, the losing team in each debate round is eliminated from the tournament, until there are only two teams left in each division. The winner of the final round in each division is considered the tournament champion for that division.

During preliminary rounds, probably the only people present will be you, your opponents, and the judge. However, people do watch elimination rounds. If you've been eliminated, then watch and flow some of the elimination debates. If you're out of the tournament, then you've got something to learn from the people who are still in it!

Most tournaments have both preliminary and elimination rounds. However, in a **round robin** tournament, you debate against every other team in a preliminary-round-only competition. Most round robins don't have elimination rounds. Also, some league tournaments and scrimmages use preliminary rounds only. On the other hand, some tournaments use an elimination-only format. The most common elimination-only format is the two-loss, or double-elimination, system. As soon as a team loses two rounds, they are eliminated. Tournament format varies depending on what purpose the tournament is serving.

How many tournaments do I have to go to per year?

How many tournaments you compete in is up to you. Some very motivated debaters go to six to eight per semester. Some debaters go to one or two. Of course, you should never consider jeopardizing your schoolwork to go to more debate tournaments. Every coach knows that you are a student first and a debater second. If you are having trouble balancing schoolwork with debate work, please talk to your coach. He or she wants to help you succeed at all of your academic endeavors. As a different consideration, keep in mind that your school may have limited money for debate, so you may find that you want to go to more tournaments than are available. The real question usually ends up being, "How many do I get to go to?" I know that the hard-working debaters who take going to tournaments seriously are the ones on the short list for the next tournament.

What formal rules are there in debate?

This book describes four different **formats** of debate, but there are many more. Each format has different time limits and traditions. However, the differences are minor. Almost any debate concept described can apply in any format. In the following time limit tables, the Cs are for constructives, and Rs for rebuttals. *CXer* is the cross-examiner. *CXed* is the respondent. Each speaker's speeches are listed in his or her column, along with the times.

Classic debate

AFFIRMATIVE		TIME	NEGATIVE	
1st SPKR	2nd SPKR		1st SPKR	2nd SPKR
AC		6 mins		
CXed		3 mins	CXer	
		6 mins	NC	
	CXer	3 mins	CXed	
		5 mins		1NR
CXer		3 mins		CXed
	1AR	7 mins		
	CXed	3 mins		CXer
		5 mins	2NR	
2AR		4 mins		
		3 mins		Summary
	Summary	3 mins		

Despite its name, this is a new format of debate invented and used in Minnesota. The intention is to return to older debate traditions and conventions to make debate more appealing to a wider variety of high school students. This means that counterplans and critiques are not as welcome as on-case negative attacks. Two topics are used per semester. Topics tend toward general policy.

Classic debate is unique among debate formats in that preparation time is fixed for each speaker and is not at a speaker's discretion. After the 1NR, each speaker gets two minutes of prep time before his or her speech.

For more information on the Classic debate format, navigate to http://www.mdta.org.

Cross-examination (CX)

AFFIRMATIVE		TIME	NEGATIVE	
Ist SPKR	2nd SPKR		Ist SPKR	2nd SPKR
IAC		8 mins		
CXed		3 mins		CXer
		8 mins	INC	
CXer		3 mins	CXed	
	2AC	8 mins		
	CXed	3 mins	CXer	
		8 mins		2NC
	CXer	3 mins		CXed
		5 mins	INR	
IAR		5 mins		
		5 mins		2NR
	2AR	5 mins		

Cross-examination debate is the oldest format still practiced in the U.S. today. Topics last the whole academic year. Because of this, CX is the most research-intensive debate format: constructives are typically 95% evidence.

In this format, the 2NC and 1NR are back-to-back and treated as a single unit, called the **negative block**. The two negative speakers divide the issues, which means the 1NR is treated as if it were another constructive. This puts an enormous time pressure on the 1AR. Each team is usually given 5, 8, or 10 minutes of preparation time to use at their discretion.

The N.F.H.S. selects the annual high school topics: http://www.nfhs.org.

The National Debate Tournament and Cross-Examination Debate Association select college topics: http://www.cedadebate .org. In college, constructives are 9 minutes and rebuttals are 6 minutes.

Parliamentary (Parli)

GOVERNMENT		TIME	OPPOSITION	
Prime Minister	Government Minister		Leader of Opposition	Opposition Member
1st Gov. C		7 mins		
		8 mins	1st Opp. C	
	2nd Gov. C	8 mins		
		8 mins		2nd Opp. C
		4 mins	Opp. R	
Gov. R		5 mins		

The parliamentary format has been gaining popularity in the U.S. at both the high school and college level. Parli is the only debate format where direct quotation is not allowed. Debaters may make indirect references to research and cite expert opinion (analytic briefs) but may not read cards. In an effort to encourage general knowledge of current events rather than specific topic knowledge, topics are used for one round only. Furthermore, debaters get the topic only 15 minutes before the round begins. The emphasis is on extemporaneous speaking, not research.

Parli is also the only debate format with no preparation time in the round. Furthermore, it does not have official cross-examination periods. There are **points of information** (POI) instead: debaters ask their opponents questions in the middle of speeches. A debater stands up, waits for his opponent's acknowledgment (which the speaker may decline to do), and then asks his question. Whether you're asking or responding, politeness is key. The bottom line is that the debate runs without interruption; finding "virtual" preparation time is vital.

The U.S. college organizations are A.P.D.A. (http://apdaweb.org) and the N.P.D.A. (http://www.parlidebate.org). To my knowledge, Oregon is the only state with high school parliamentary debate: http://www.speechoregon.com.

Public Forum (PF)

FIRST TEAM		TIME	SECOND TEAM	
1ˢᵗ SPKR	2ⁿᵈ SPKR		1ˢᵗ SPKR	2ⁿᵈ SPKR
I - C		4 mins		
		4 mins	I - C	
CF		3 mins	CF	
	2 - C	4 mins		
		4 mins		2 - C
	CF	3 mins		CF
I - R		2 mins		
		2 mins	I - R	
GCF		3 mins	GCF	
	2 - R	I min		
		I min		2 - R

The public forum format was invented in the U.S. in the late 1990s to interest the general public. In fact, PF has been nicknamed "Ted Turner debate" after the popular founder of C.N.N. Although evidence is allowed, topics last only one month, so in-depth research is not a priority. Topics are policy resolutions, but Affirmatives are not supposed to advocate a formal policy, nor should Negatives advocate counterplans.

Unique among formats, the Negative might end up speaking first. Before the round, teams flip a coin to determine which side speaks first. Also, PF has **cross-fire** (CF): bi-directional cross-examination. Both sides can ask and answer questions. The idea is that debaters politely take turns. Please also note that the third cross-fire, the grand cross-fire (GCF), involves all four debaters asking and answering in turn.

For more information about the format, check out the N.S.D.A. at http://www.speechanddebate.org.

Review questions:

1. Why is there almost always a novice division at a debate tournament?

2. Define "bye," "preliminary round," "elimination round," and "round robin tournament."

3. What are the speech times in your format?

4. How is cross-examination handled in your format?

5. What are the rules and expectations about evidence in your format?

6. Are there any rules or expectations about kinds of argument that are disallowed or discouraged in your format?

Milestone:

You should be getting ready for your first tournament!

How do I adapt to my judges and win my rounds?

All debaters would like to know the preferences of their judges
before rounds so that they can adapt. Most tournaments do allow
judges to give pre-round advice to explain their feelings about debate. However, every judge wants to see good arguments about
whatever you want to argue, so every judge tries to be open-
minded. Here is a good technique: ask the judge if there's anything
you can do to give her or him a more pleasurable round to watch.
You'll get a sense of the speaking and debating style the judge prefers. Adapting your delivery is the most important part of adapta-
tion. There are three common judge types you will encounter:

1. Flow
2. Communication
3. Lay

These three couldn't have more different preferences for speaking
style, and you speak in a way that irritates them at your own risk.

The flow-centric judge tends to care little about delivery. His
or her focus is the line-by-line. For this type of judge, you can
usually go fast, bring up many different issues, and try ideas that
are new and experimental. Of course, you'll need to present overviews that explain the whole round, but the judge's concern will
be your argumentation and evidence.

The second type of judge, a communication judge, prefers a more traditional style. He is less interested in the flow and more interested in the overviews and persuasion. For this judge, it is important to bring up fewer issues, to speak more slowly and clearly, and to focus on the overall presentation of the round. While this type of judge makes decisions holistically, you can't ignore the line-by-line. You need to make both solid overview and line-by-line argumentation, but the emphasis should be on the overviews and persuasion if you want to win in front of this type of judge.

So what's a lay judge?

A lay judge is one who has no experience judging or debating. These are people who have been pulled in from off the street because the tournament was short-handed. While we all would prefer that every judge have at least some experience, every debater gets lay judges from time to time. It's important to know how to adapt:

1. The lay judge will almost never vote on any procedural arguments. Don't bother.

2. Split complicated ideas into smaller components. Expert judges are familiar with the topic and debate theory and can handle larger, more complicated chunks of information. For lay judges, they need small, bite-sized pieces of information. Use lots of logical connectors, like "Spending hurts the economy," explain it thoroughly, then read a card; "Hard to believe, but this would hurt the economy so badly that it could trigger an international crisis," explain it thoroughly, then read another card; "In fact, this international crisis might even be so bad that it could engulf the world in war: all the way from a simple budget deficit to a risk of world war," then read your final card. It's like giving extended versions of tags. Start at a level of information that seems a very basic part of the argument— then go one simpler. Lay judges won't follow the chain of logic unless you help them out.

3. Spend more time on what you're winning than what you're losing. For example, the Affirmative should devote serious

time to case but should spend very little time on negative off-case positions. This is, of course, backwards from what you'd do with an experienced judge. Good judges can tell that you're winning a position even when you cover it quickly, and they remember that you've won it when they make their decision. Lay judges tend to notice only whether they agree or disagree with you as you're speaking. Defensive arguments taint a lay judge's perception; spending a lot of time defensively answering your opponent's position may lead a lay judge to falsely conclude that you're on the defensive because you're losing overall. That's why when you do answer your opponent's positions, you should make one or two _offensive_ arguments against it (a link turn, if you can) rather than several defensive arguments.

4. Roadmap and signpost. It is vital to winning over the lay judge. They very well might not flow at all. They may write down a few notes to keep track of who's saying what but not follow the detailed evolution of the argument. And, of course, you should speak more slowly for a lay judge. You may even need to trim cards shorter to fit all your arguments in. If lay judges don't feel lost when you're speaking, then they'll vote for you.

5. Connect it back to the ballot. Lay judges may be overwhelmed by what they're hearing. They might understand the issues, and they may even have an opinion as to which side is winning each position, but they probably will not know how to relate this to who wins. If you can give them a clear understanding of how the arguments apply to their ballot, "Therefore, if we win this, we win the round. But if we lose it, then we lose," then lay judges will be more inclined to vote for you. Although I listed this idea under adapting to lay judges, this is good advice for any judge.

That's fine, but I really want to know is how to adapt my arguments to my judge's political views.

Never, ever do this. Judges are supposed to be open-minded. It's not whether they agree with you; all that matters is whether you made good arguments. If you switch to a case or position that you aren't as familiar with in the hopes that the judge likes it more, you are likely to make worse arguments because you are on a position that makes you uncomfortable or that you don't know as well. And more philosophically, I think it's wrong to adapt your arguments this way. I would call it self-censorship. Debate is supposed to be about the free exchange of ideas. Adapt in style, not in substance.

But I heard the advanced students on my team talking about adapting arguments to the judge's paradigm. What's a paradigm?

People tend to blow this word out of all proportion and act like it's a super-complicated concept. It's not. A **paradigm** (pronounced PAIR-uh-DIME) is an overarching theory, as simple as that. In debate, a paradigm is an overarching theory about what a fair debate round should look like. In other words, it's a kind of blueprint for debaters to know what kinds of procedural arguments matter. It is acceptable to say, "I want to make this argument as a counterplan, but this judge dislikes counterplans. Maybe I could turn it into a disadvantage..." You're not changing what arguments you make, merely the theory you present them with. It is acceptable to ask a judge about his or her paradigm before the round begins. In effect, all you're doing is trying to realize your judge's ideal round, or paradigm, while making your preferred arguments.

In each paradigm, the primary question is which side has the burden of proof for what kinds of argument. For example, a stock issues judge would put the burden of proof on the Negative to show that a critique is an acceptable form of argumentation; for a *tabula rasa* judge, the burden of proof is on the team claiming that the critique isn't acceptable. This idea of burden of proof is closely tied to **presumption**. Presumption is the concept about who should win if there's a tie—and presumption is applied so differently in each paradigm that it's not a uniform concept that can be covered as such. Don't worry about trying to parse whether you have presumption or not; few debate rounds are ever decided on it.

What are the basic paradigms?

1. Tabula rasa

2. Hypo-testing
3. Policymaker
4. Stock issues
5. Games

There are other types of judging paradigms, but they far less common than these.

The tabula rasa paradigm is the easiest to understand. A tabula rasa judge does not want to **intervene**, that is, not insert his or her own preferences into the round. The tabula rasa judge leaves it all up to the debaters to decide; he sees himself as a blank slate waiting to be inscribed by the debaters' arguments. There are limits to the blankness of the slate, however. You would never successfully argue:

1. that you should have more speech and prep time than your opponent or than the tournament rules give you; that a rebuttal should turn into a constructive (that is, make new arguments) or a speech should become a cross-examination (that is, interrupt an opponent's speech);

2. that you can debate a different topic than the one the tournament assigns even if both sides agree to a new topic or that you can flip affirmative/negative sides with your opponent from what the tournament assigns even if both teams want to flip sides;

3. that the judge should not assign a winner and a loser, or that the judge should make his or her decision on any basis other than the arguments made in the debate (that you're having a bad day is irrelevant to any judge).

You can make arguments about anything else except these three things, which means that everything else in this whole book is merely a suggestion to the tabula rasa judge.

A hypo-testing paradigm is also open to many arguments. This kind of judge likes to see the case treated as a truth statement that is being tested in the round, like a social scientist evaluating different theories about policy. This kind of judge is unique because she is willing to accept multiple cases within the same round. The Affirmative could run two plans if it desired and win with either one.

The policy-maker sees his job as producing the best possible policy; she accepts fiat and may be skeptical of critiques and sometimes even procedural arguments.

The stock issues paradigm is the most traditional. The stock issues judge likes to see cases written with clear stock issues and prefers that the Negative use case attacks only. This kind of judge does not like disadvantages, counterplans, or critiques but usually feels that topicality is acceptable to debate.

Finally, the games paradigm is the strangest. This kind of judge simply likes to be entertained and is willing to vote on such arguments as *Plan is bad for debate because it isn't fun to watch.* With this paradigm, the judge might even ignore the three rules no tabula rasa judge would. Who cares about time limits when we're having fun?

Someone mentioned reading poetry and playing music during a debate. What paradigm is this?

These are **performance** or narrative cases. In this type of case, the Affirmative presents a case that is based not on the evidence of expert quotations but on non-fiction or fiction stories, or narratives, or on poetry or music that the Affirmative performs. That's right—your opponent may begin rapping a case at you.

How do you respond? Well, if your opponent is using the stories or poems or whatever to support a traditional case, then treat it like any other case. If you got a poem instead of a quotation to show how bad nuclear war is, then you can treat it like you would any other evidence: poke holes in it. In this instance, it's really a stylistic difference rather than a whole new paradigm of a debate round, however weird it may feel.

On the other hand, your opponent might make arguments like *The only way to know things is through song* or *Experts and quotations are all liars and lies.* In this case, you have two choices: you can concede these arguments, ditch your evidence, and make up your own songs; or you can beat these arguments. I recommend the latter.

Another school of thought believes that the language you use in the round, your rhetoric, is part of your advocacy. Remember from Chapter 1 the difference between argumentation versus advocacy. However, judges in this paradigm believe that there is no distinction between argumentation and advocacy. In other words, these judges believe that the Affirmative is not advocating only its text; the Affirmative is also advocating every word or argument that it speaks. This means that you can lose even if your plan is a good idea, even if it is fair, if only you happen to use a word that is offensive. If you do use such a word, the Negative can run a language "critique" on you. The Affirmative can run language critique against the Negative, too. Such arguments are not actually critiques. Languages critiques are much more similar to procedural arguments in structure except that the voting issue is *Offensive language should be punished with a loss*. I prefer to call them rhetorical arguments to remind us that they need a voting issue about how rhetoric affects debate, like procedural arguments must have, rather than an implication about how the framework is bad, like real critiques.

Can I actually lose because of bad language?

Yes, many judges do believe that rhetorical arguments are voting issues. It's hard to imagine voting for a debater that, though clearly better, is also clearly racist. It all depends on what your vision of an ideal debate round looks like. If you think there are limits to what can be said by the debaters, then you will believe there should be a procedural limit on rhetoric. Many judges, including me, believe that any procedural limit on rhetoric will have a chilling effect. I'm willing to accept the very rare chance of racist language because I think the alternative is to make the debaters too conscious about their words, leading to self-censorship.

For example, many teams gender-neutralize their evidence. They read through all their cards and cut out offending pronouns, turning "he" into "s/he" and "man" into "human." This is hard enough to do, but the danger to me is that debaters choose to forgo whole topics of conversation because certain authors are impossible to sanitize or because the subject itself might offend. I believe in the free exchange of ideas; I want a debate round where everything is on the table for discussion. If you're easily offended, wear a helmet.

The problem is that rhetorical arguments don't stop with the blatantly offensive (racist, sexist, etc.). For example, some teams have run rhetorical arguments about the verb "to be." The argument is that "to be" in all its forms, such as "Jane is a woman," causes us to think very categorically and clouds our understanding of the world. "Jane <u>acts</u> like a woman," is really what we mean to say. Perhaps there's some validity to it, but is it really a reason to vote against a team? For me, the most I will ever do if I believe a team has won its rhetorical argument is to punish a speaker's points. If someone says racist words in my round, he or she will receive zero points. But I might also have to give that same debater the win. If you can convince me that you deserve to win, in spite of using awful rhetoric, then so be it. Other judges have a different paradigm than mine that is more open to rhetorical arguments as voting issues.

So what happens if I disagree with my judge's decision? Should I argue with him?

It's unlikely to do much good: no judge is going to change a decision because you try to intimidate him or her. Think of it this way: your judge is an ethical human being who's trying to make the best, fairest decision. Judges don't want to make an arbitrary decision; they had some reason for making it. Even if you don't buy their reason, it's something to consider for next time. Usually, it's a matter of perspective: you think you were clear about something, but the judge didn't find what you said to be clear at all. If this is the case, it's your fault for not speaking more clearly. Too many debaters forget, become arrogant, and resent the judge. Listen, ask questions, and respect your judge, who deserves at least that—even if it's too much to respect the judge's decision. Plus you don't want to get a reputation as a sore loser. The debate community is small, and sore losers make it even smaller.

So it looks like that's everything.

Not by a long shot, but now you know all the basic theory, logic, and skills. Don't think that just because you know the basics that the learning has stopped. This book has only cursorily brushed upon the tip of the iceberg. There's a lot more to learn, and the best way to learn it is to keep asking questions. Getting beaten isn't a tragedy, but considering your knowledge complete is.

Debate is about asking questions and learning, not arguing without reflection. Win or lose, you should try to learn from each round. If you win, be a gracious winner. If you lose, be a gracious loser. It's vital that you understand that there is such a thing as a good loss when you competed against a very strong opponent and performed to the utmost of your ability. These are educational and character building. Understand that no two wins will ever be the same; keep learning and adapting. That's what becoming a debater is about: continuing to learn at every opportunity. Whatever else you do, please have fun and keep at it!

You sure had a lot to say about debate.

Well, I am passionate about it. I tried to be succinct as possible.

Yeah... not really. But it was good information.

Oh well. Anyway, if you ever see me on the circuit, please feel free to come up and say "hi." Good debating!

Review questions:

1. How do you adapt to a lay judge?

2. How do you adapt to a communication judge?

3. How do you adapt to a flow judge?

4. Explain the five judging paradigms you might encounter.

5. What are some arguments for and against performance cases?

6. What are some arguments for and against language critiques?

Milestone:

Take the time to reflect on every round! Analyze what worked, what didn't, and what you can do to improve. And you should check out my other book, *Statistics for Debaters and Extempers*, on lulu.com. It's an appropriate next resource for intermediate debaters to read.

Index

Index

Made in the USA
San Bernardino, CA
28 August 2016